SHORT CUTS
for busy dressmakers

SHORT CUTS
for busy dressmakers

Ann Ladbury

B.T. Batsford Ltd, London

First published 1980
© Ann Ladbury 1980
Reprinted in paperback 1989
All rights reserved. No part of this publication may
be reproduced, in any form or by any means, without
permission from the publishers.
ISBN 0 7134 6321 X
Typeset by Tek-Art Ltd, West Wickham, Kent
Printed by Courier International Ltd
Tiptree, Essex
for the publishers B.T. Batsford Ltd,
4 Fitzhardinge Street, London W1H 0AH

Contents

Introduction

This book is really about saving time; about how to sew successfully but yet not spend too long on it.

Why are we in a hurry? Why do we want to produce things in less time than it once took? Because our whole existence and the framework of life is different. More activities are open to us and we want to take part in many of them. Not long ago the chance to play various sports or to attend social functions and entertainments was open to relatively few. So our time has to be re-allocated but not I hope at the expense of such an enjoyable and economical activity as sewing.

Everyone, from time to time, wants something in a hurry. Even I, steeped in the craft and its traditions, have to choose a pattern that is easy, fabric that won't be any trouble, and avoid lengthy processes when I am short of time and need an outfit quickly. And how I bless such things as Wundaweb and Velcro to help me. I have chosen processes for the book that make good practical use of the aids available to us and I have packed in lots of tips too. The contents are confined to processes of two kinds: those that are quick to do and those that can be time-consuming but cannot always be avoided. For the latter I have described how I work them in a quick, easy way.

There are a number of reasons besides lack of time for which short cuts in sewing are sought. I hope one of them is not a desire to lower standards. Not only is that obviously undesirable and very short-sighted, but it is unnecessary. Taking a short cut or using an aid or a gadget does not have to equate with inferior results — all the things I suggest in this book make for excellent results.

Where the following reasons for adopting short cuts are concerned, it is in all cases a very good thing to take advantage of a quicker or easier method.

Limited skill

With all crafts it is necessary to practise in order to be skilful. If you haven't done very much sewing or if the things you have made have been spaced out in time you should avoid complicated processes and styles. You may reach the limit of your interest in pursuing the craft, but happily, fashion is such that it is easy to be well clad without having to make classic outfits.

Loss of interest

If your sewing takes a long time and you don't seem to be getting anywhere, it is easy to lose interest. Quick, successful results that you can wear will encourage you to go on.

Lack of confidence

Your confidence may have been sapped earlier by mistakes at school, by a mother who can make anything or you may just be the sort who is not relaxed with practical things. Adjust your approach to consider the few actions you need to take in order to make something, not the many; consider also the little time it will take if you adopt some short cuts.

Lack of experience

Limited sewing experience means limited knowledge of handling different fabrics; making a range of simple garments is a quick way to increase your knowledge.

All the designs in Part Two provide you with the chance to increase your skill and confidence while making things to wear. Choose from the fabrics suggested and use the processes in Part One and you can't go wrong.

PART ONE
Processes & techniques

General tips

Use a medium to large machine stitch, not a small one.

If the fabric wrinkles or puckers when you begin machining, put a piece of tissue paper or old pattern pieces underneath.

Avoid fabrics like checks that take a long time to lay out and prepare.

Plain fabrics show every stitch and seam line; small prints and patterns are easier.

Avoid processes where you went wrong last time. Practise those when you have plenty of time.

It is actually quicker to use the iron on each process as you work. When complete, the garment needs only a quick press.

Always have the iron out when sewing.

Don't hurry the pressing. An extra 20 seconds spent now is worth 2 minutes of frustration later.

Think of the iron as a sewing aid; use it before you stitch as well as afterwards.

Avoid close-fitting styles; they will take longer to fit.

It is easier to make a top and skirt, if you have fitting problems, than a dress.

When attaching wide braid press it in position with strips of Wundaweb which do not need to be tacked and which make it firmer.

Attach braid or ribbon with one row of machine stitching down the centre.

Choose loose styles drawn in with a belt, elastic, etc.

If you choose fabric that frays, make sure you have a bottle of Fray-Check by you as you sew.

When using pile fabrics or those with a one-way pattern, mark a chalk arrow on the wrong side of each piece after cutting out, so that you will see clearly the direction in which to stitch.

Eliminate clearing up — spread an old sheet, piece of plastic or even newspapers on the floor round the machine and working area to catch the bits.

Jersey and knits are easy to sew provided you choose the correct processes.

Where appropriate choose border fabrics or those with ready-hemmed edges to save time.

Needlecord and cotton velveteen are not difficult to sew, contrary to general opinion.

Velvets with woven backing and deep pile are very difficult to sew.

Velour is easy to sew.

Panne velvet is not difficult to sew.

Buy white cotton fringing and dye it any colour.

Buy white or écru crochet edgings and inserts and dye any colour.

Buy two silky dressing gown girdles in different colours and twist to make into a belt.

Remember that most fabrics need to be softened with steam in order to press them properly.

Instead of pinning down a pattern, place a couple of things on it to weight it while you chalk round the edge. Remove pattern to cut out.

If threads slip and elude you, lick your fingers for a better grip.

When stitching a bias seam use a slight zig-zag stitch to keep the 'give' in the seam.

Reinforce the top of a slit seam by placing a folded piece of ribbon or tape under the final few machine stitches.

When applying binding ease it on round concave edges but stretch it to go round convex curves.

Twill weave braid — the sort without a selvedge — is a good substitute for binding.

If you are stitching to a V, start at the point and stitch outwards; return to the point and stitch the other side.

1 Pockets

If you don't want to omit pockets completely either because you need them or because they form part of a style feature, choose one of the following types.

POCKETS FOR USE

Vertical seam pocket

This is the easiest type of pocket to make; it is not visible and you can use it. The seam pocket can be added to any garment and placed in any convenient position. Its only disadvantage is that it can become floppy and wrinkled but this is overcome by using interfacing to keep it flat.

The pocket bag is an oval shape angled from a straight vertical edge 22 cm long. If you have to cut your own, draw round your hand to obtain the right shape and size.

Cut out once in soft iron-on Vilene and twice in fabric for each pocket. If the fabric is bulky cut one piece in cotton lawn, nylon jersey or lining fabric.

Press the interfacing to the wrong side of a piece of fabric (not the lining piece). This is the back section of the pocket.

On the garment mark the pocket opening in the seam 16 cm in length. Machine the seam from hem to lower chalk mark and from the upper mark to the top of the garment, reversing the stitching to fasten off at each end of the pocket opening. Adjust the machine to the longest stitch and machine the length of the pocket opening. Press the seams open (fig 1.1).

Place the back pocket bag to seam allowance of back of garment, with right sides together, and machine, taking no more than 5 mm seam allowance (fig 1.2).

Fig 1.2

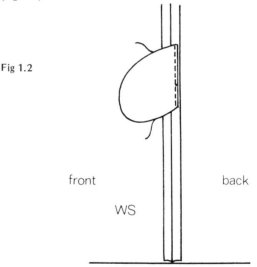

front   back

WS

Fig 1.1

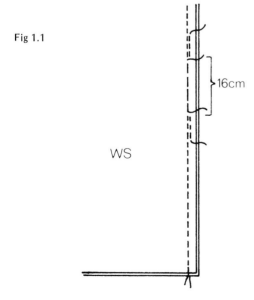

16cm

WS

Attach the front pocket (it may be lining) to the front in the same way. Press open the seams.

Re-press the back pocket so that it extends towards the front of the garment and lies on top of the front pocket piece. Snip the seam allowance on the back of the garment level with the end of the pocket, at the top and bottom. Neaten the edges of the garment seams.

Pin the pocket pieces together, inserting the pins well within the outer edge. Using tailor's chalk, mark the shape of the bag, drawing a line from the seam at the top of the pocket opening, round the outer edge and finishing at the garment seam. Machine on this line.

Remove pins. Trim the edges to 5 mm and zig-zag over the two edges to neaten (fig 1.3).

Fig 1.3

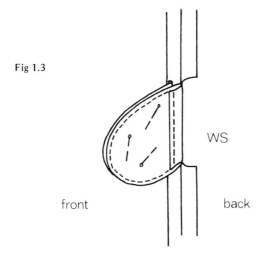

WS

front   back

Cut a piece of Wundaweb 12 cm long and slip it under the pocket at the front. Push it into the fold at the seam between the garment and the pocket to hold the pocket in position. Press well to melt the adhesive. Remove the large machine stitches in the seam (fig 1.4).

Fig 1.4

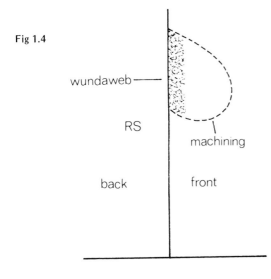

wundaweb

RS

machining

back   front

TIP If you want to make a feature of the pocket, baste it to the garment, draw a chalk line on the right side within the edge of the pocket and machine.

Horizontal seam pocket

If you have a yoke seam on a shirt, jacket, skirt or trousers, a pocket can easily be inserted. Begin by cutting a piece of Vilene exactly to the size of the bag. This will vary according to the position of the garment. Pin it to the right side of the garment and trim to size, making sure the edges will not interfere with processes to be worked later. This is the pattern.

Cut one piece of lining fabric the same size as the Vilene but adding 1 cm seam allowance all round. Cut a piece of garment fabric but make it 3 cm deeper than the lining. Cut a piece of soft iron-on Vilene the same size as the fabric and press it to the wrong side (fig 1.5).

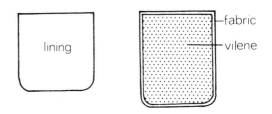

lining   fabric

vilene

Fig 1.5

Stitch the garment yoke seam but leave a gap where the pocket is to go. The gap should be the width of the original Vilene pattern. Alter your machine to its biggest stitch and stitch across the pocket opening. Press the seam open, neaten the edges and add top stitching if you wish (fig 1.6).

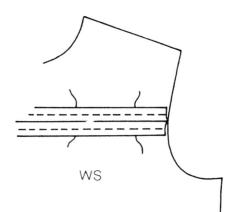

WS

Fig 1.6

On the wrong side put the piece of pocket lining to the lower yoke seam allowance with right sides together. Machine 3 mm from the edge. Press so that the pocket lining hangs down (fig 1.7).

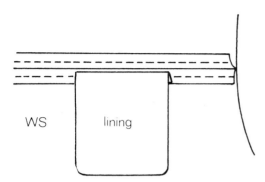

Fig 1.7

Put the interfaced fabric right-side down on top of the first piece with the edge level with the edge of the upper seam allowance on the yoke. Machine the two together 3 mm from the edge. Neaten the pocket edge by working zig-zag stitch over both edges (fig 1.8).

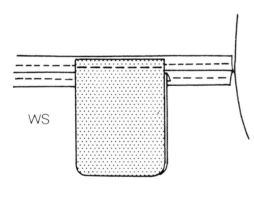

Fig 1.8

Pin the pieces of pocket bag together. Mark the size and shape of the pocket with tailor's chalk or with pencil if chalk is not visible on the Vilene. Machine round the bag, trim the turnings to 5 mm and neaten both edges together. Where the bag crosses the yoke seam, herringbone the edges of the bag to the seam allowances. Remove pins, press well and remove the large machine stitches in the seam (fig 1.9).

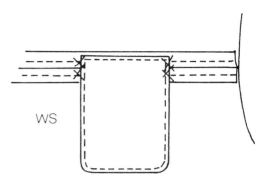

Fig 1.9

Patch pocket

This is mainly decorative with limited functional use, simply because things make it bulge. Decide on the best size and position by cutting a piece of Vilene and pinning it on the garment in various places and at different angles, trimming the Vilene until you are satisfied. This is the pattern.

Cut a piece of soft iron-on Vilene 4 cm deeper than the experimental pocket. Cut a piece of fabric the same size. Cut one more piece 4 cm shorter than the Vilene. These three pieces will make one pocket. If the fabric is bulky cut the smaller piece from cotton lawn, lining material or nylon jersey (fig 1.10).

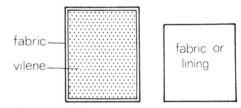

Fig 1.10

Place the lining piece to pocket piece right sides together with top edges level and machine, taking 5 mm seam allowance. Press the turnings open if both layers are fabric, press towards lining if the smaller piece is made of lighter fabric (fig 1.11).

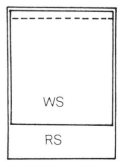

Fig 1.11

Bring the three raw edges of pocket and lining together, insert pins round the outside, well within the outer edges. The lining is smaller than the pocket so you will have to force the edges to meet (fig 1.12).

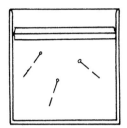

Fig 1.12

Using tailor's chalk and a ruler, chalk a line on which to stitch. Mark a gap 4 cm long in one side through which to turn the pocket. If the pocket has curved corners use the paper pattern, or original Vilene pocket, as a guide to marking accurate pairs of curves.

Machine all three sides, reversing at the top and at each side of the gap (fig 1.13).

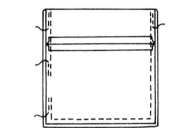

Fig 1.13

Remove pins. Trim raw edges to 3 mm and cut off the corners. Press the stitching flat. Push the pocket through the gap and turn it right-side out. Roll the corners and edges and press the edge from the lining side. Press the raw edges inwards at the gap.

Edge stitch all round the outer edge of the pocket. Machine again across the top 2 cm down from the top edge. Press (fig 1.14).

Fig 1.14

Place pocket in position on the right side of the garment, anchor with two pins. Baste the pocket across the top and then round the other three sides. Do not remove the pins.

Machine, starting at the edge level with the lower row of machining, stitch at an angle up to the top of the pocket, swivel the work, stitch along the top for three stitches, swivel and stitch round the pocket parallel with the edge. At the second corner repeat the triangle (fig 1.15).

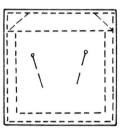

Fig 1.15

Remove pins and basting. Fasten off machine ends. Press well on both right *and wrong* sides of pocket.

> **TIPS** Edge stitch the pocket and leave your machine set on that stitch; don't do any more sewing before stitching the pocket in position. This will ensure two rows of identical stitching.
>
> When making the strengthening triangles at the top of the pocket count the stitches as you work the first one and make the second corner identical.

Double patch pocket

If you require two patch pockets, one above the other, the quickest way to do them is to make one and divide it with machine stitching.

Cut a piece of fabric the width of the lower pocket and long enough to extend from the top pocket position right down to the base of the lower pocket. Add 3 cm hem allowance at the top and 1.5 cm round the other sides.

Neaten round all four sides. Turn in the top edge 3 cm and press. Slip a piece of Wundaweb under the edge and press well. Machine on the edge across the top and again 2 cm below and parallel (fig 1.16).

Turn in and tack the other three sides of the pocket. Tack and press. At the edge that will be nearest to the side seam slip a strip of Wundaweb, cut to 1 cm wide, under the edge and press. The strip should be about 18 cm in length (fig 1.17).

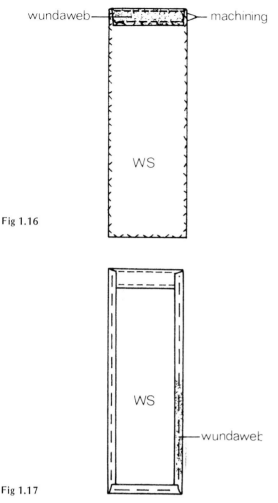

wundaweb — machining

WS

Fig 1.16

WS

wundaweb

Fig 1.17

Place the pocket on the right side of the garment and pin in position. Baste across the top and round all edges. Machine in place all round but leaving a space of 12 cm where the Wundaweb has been

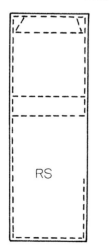

RS

Fig 1.18

inserted. Stitch up from the corner for 6-8 cm then stop. Start again 12 cm above and continue to the top. Stitch triangles at the top corners as described for the previous patch pocket (fig 1.18).

Using tailor's chalk, rule two parallel lines across the pocket, one to mark the base of the top pocket, the other to mark the top of the lower pocket. Machine on these lines. Fasten off all ends of machining. Remove pins and tacking and press well on both sides (fig 1.19).

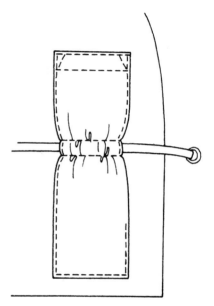

Fig 1.19

> **TIP** If the garment has a belt, make a slot for it by stitching the parallel lines described above at waist level. Mark these lines before attaching the pocket to the garment and do not stitch across the ends of the belt slot.

POCKETS FOR DECORATION

Pockets which involve cutting the fabric take a long time to do properly. If you want the effect that a flap or a welt provides make them purely decorative.

Cut a piece of Vilene to the shape of a flap or welt and pin it to the garment in various positions, trimming it until you are satisfied. This is the pattern.

Flap

Cut a piece of soft iron-on Vilene to size allowing 1 cm seam allowance all round. Cut two pieces of fabric the same size, or, if the fabric is bulky, cut one piece in lining fabric. Trim 2 mm off the outer edges of the lining or under piece of the flap. Press the Vilene to the wrong side of the outer piece (fig 1.20).

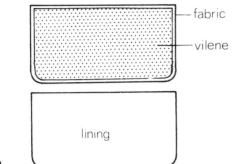

fabric

vilene

lining

Fig 1.20

Place flap and lining right sides together making the edges meet. Tack together. Machine across the ends and along the bottom, taking 1 cm seam allowance. Chalk a line on which to stitch, especially if the flap has rounded corners (fig 1.21). Remove

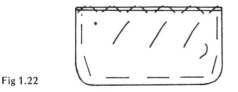

Fig 1.21

tackings and trim turnings to 5 mm and cut off the corners or snip the curves. Turn flap right-side out and roll edges. Press on both sides. Baste along the flap to hold the layers together. The flap will be slightly curled inwards due to the fact that the lining was smaller (fig 1.22).

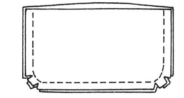

Fig 1.22

Trim the raw edges at the top of the flap to 3 mm and neaten the edges together. Press.

Place the flap on the garment upside-down and right-side down with the neatened edge in what will be the position for the top of the flap. Baste to the garment. Machine flap to garment, placing the stitching 3 mm in from the neatened edge. Remove tacking,

roll flap down so that it is right-side up and tack firmly below the join. Press well and stitch by machine or hand 5 mm below the join. Press again (fig 1.23).

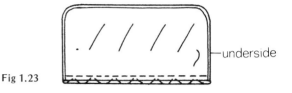

underside

Fig 1.23

Finish by sewing a button through the centre of the flap and the garment, or insert a metal-capped press stud (fig 1.24).

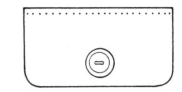

Fig 1.24

Welt

A welt is a rectangle, usually fairly narrow. Using an experimental welt cut in Vilene, cut a piece of fabric double the width plus 1 cm seam allowance all round. Cut a piece of soft iron-on interfacing the same size and press it to the wrong side of the fabric (fig 1.25).

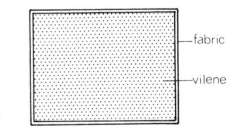

fabric

vilene

Fig 1.25

Trim a little off the ends of the welt at an angle, starting halfway along the side and graduating to 2 mm at the raw edge of the welt (fig 1.26).

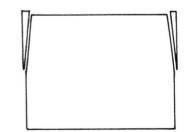

Fig 1.26

Fold welt right sides together, make the ends meet and pin. Machine across the ends taking a 1 cm turning. Trim edges to 5 mm and cut off the corners (fig 1.27).

Fig 1.27

Turn welt right-side out and roll the ends. Press. Baste across the welt to hold the layers together. The welt will be slightly curled. Trim raw edges to 3 mm and neaten (fig 1.28).

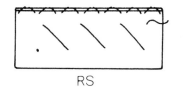

Fig 1.28

Pin welt in position on the garment with right-side down and below the position it will be in when finished. The neatened edge should be at the top. Tack to the garment. Machine along the welt 3 mm below the edge. Remove tackings (fig 1.29).

Fig 1.29

Roll welt over so that it is right-side up. Tack welt to the garment just above the join, tack the top edge and tack across the ends. Slip stitch the welt ends to the garment by hand, then machine across the ends 4 mm from the edge and along the bottom 4 mm above the join (fig 1.30).

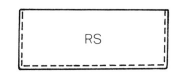

Fig 1.30

TIPS When attaching the flap or welt to the garment, begin machining at the centre and stitch to the end, turn and stitch to the far end, turn and stitch back to the middle. This prevents movement of the flap as you stitch.

When you machine don't stitch right to the end, stop and turn 2 mm before the end. This prevents the stitching from showing when the flap is folded into position.

Use Fold-a-Band inside the welt; the edges give you an accurate stitching line. Cut it to size, press to wrong side of fabric and cut out adding 1 cm seam allowance all round.

2 Waist finishes and belts

The choice of waist finish depends mainly on the design of the outfit. If the waist will be covered choose one of the quick finishes as follows.

ELASTIC PETERSHAM

When making skirts from knit fabric omit the zip and darts. Finish the waist edge of the skirt with zig-zag stitch. Measure elastic petersham round your waist and cut, allowing 2 cm to overlap. Lap one end over the other end, machine in a square to hold firmly.

Divide the petersham and the top of the skirt into four. Use pins to mark the skirt, but with dots made with felt pen on the petersham.

Place one edge of the petersham on the right side of the skirt, overlapping by 1 cm. Match up the four marks and pin. Have the petersham to the right and insert the pins with the heads to the right (fig 2.1).

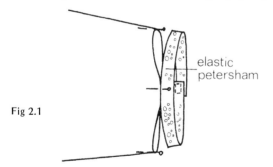

Fig 2.1

elastic petersham

Set the machine to a zig-zag stitch, begin by reversing for four stitches for strength, sew forward for four stitches then start to stretch the petersham to fit the fabric as you stitch. Remove the pins as you reach them.

Tuck the petersham into the top of the skirt and press the edge.

ELASTIC IN A CASING

If the style is suitable and the fabric light in weight the waist can be drawn in with elastic, a much quicker process than gathering the fabric into a waistband.

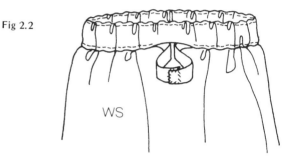

Fig 2.2

WS

Use elastic that is at least 2 cm or more wide and when cutting out the skirt, extend the pattern at the waist by twice the width of the elastic plus 1 cm. Complete the remainder of the skirt. Turn over a hem at the waist of the skirt slightly wider than the elastic, turning under the raw edge and machining it down. Leave a gap in the stitching 2 cm long for threading the elastic. In addition machine along the top edge of the skirt.

Measure the elastic round your waist, allow 2 cm to join it and cut. Sew the eye of an elastic threader to the end of the elastic and thread it through the casing.

Pull out the ends, overlap them and join by hemming securely in a square (fig 2.2).

> **TIP** Prevent the elastic from twisting as you thread it by pinning across the elastic at intervals as you pull it through. After it is in place arrange the gathering equally on the elastic and then back stitch or machine across the elastic at each side seam (fig 2.3).

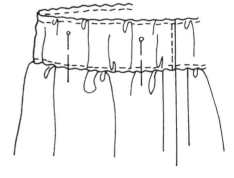

Fig 2.3

PETERSHAM

Complete the seams, darts and zip of a skirt or trousers. Measure petersham round your waist, slip the two parts of a metal clasp on the ends, fold back and pin each end of petersham so that it fits exactly when fastened. Take it off and trim the surplus ends, leaving 2 cm. Machine in a square with a zig-zag stitch beside the clasp.

Neaten the top of the skirt or trousers with zig-zag stitch. Place the edge of the petersham on to the right side of the fabric. Begin by pinning the two sections of clasp beside the zip so that they are level with the opening, then pin across the petersham at intervals round the waist. Have the petersham and the heads of the pins to the right. Remember that the petersham is at this stage upside down. If you are using curved petersham it is the convex edge that is pinned to the garment.

Work zig-zag stitch over the edge of the petersham, finishing off firmly at each end (fig 2.4). Tuck the petersham inside the skirt and press.

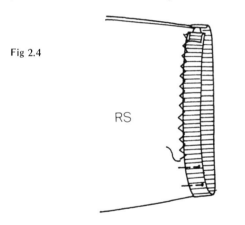

Fig 2.4

RS

WAISTBANDS

Making and attaching a waistband is time-consuming because a precisely even width has to be established and also it has to fit exactly.

> **TIPS** Measure the waistband stiffening round your waist, allow 10 cm overlap and cut. Make the waistband that length and make the trousers or skirt fit the band when you attach it.
>
> Having attached the waistband, if you find it loose snip the fabric on the inside of the band at the sides and insert a piece of elastic petersham. Pull it up to reduce the back waist and stitch the ends firmly by machining a rectangle right through the band.
>
> When making a full light-weight skirt, save time in fitting by cutting extra-long ends to the waistband (or sew ties on afterwards) adding a metre to each side of the zip. In wear the skirt is fastened then the ties are wrapped round the top and tied or buckled to size. This is also an attractive cover-up if you have inserted elastic in the top of a gathered skirt (fig 2.5).

Stiffening a waistband

There are two quick ways of stiffening a waistband.

Cut a length of petersham or waistbanding to your waist size plus 10 cm for overlapping. Place this on the wrong side of a piece of fabric, arranging it on the straight grain, and, putting a length of Wundaweb between the stiffening and the fabric, press it in position. Turn the fabric and banding over so that you can press again thoroughly from the fabric side in order to melt the Wundaweb.

Cut out the waistband fabric, allowing a seam allowance along one edge and both ends. On the other edge allow the width of the stiffening plus a seam allowance (fig 2.6).

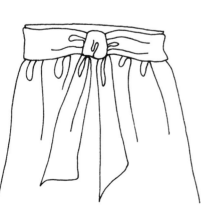

Fig 2.5

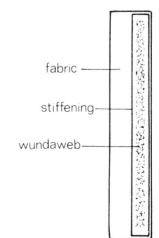

fabric

stiffening

wundaweb

Fig 2.6

The other method is to cut a piece of fabric on the straight grain to the width of heavy Fold-a-Band and long enough to fit your waist plus 10 cm for overlapping. Place Fold-a-Band on WS of fabric. Align it centrally and press.

> **TIP** A wide seam allowance is not necessary on a waistband and in fact it hampers the process of attaching it. Allow only 1 cm all round, or a little more on a thick or fraying fabric.

Attaching the waistband

Mark with chalk the 10 cm overlap at the end of the waistband. Hold the skirt or trousers *wrong-side* out and pin the overlap point on the band to match the zip or opening on the back edge of the skirt. Pin the other end to match the front edge, leaving a seam allowance extending. Pin at intervals between matching the waistband and skirt-edge seam allowances. The seam allowance on the waistband is indicated by the edge of the petersham or Fold-a-band perforations. Insert the pins vertically. Tack the band to the garment, making the stitching just beside the edge of the petersham or along perforations of Fold-a-Band. Remove the pins. Machine on the tacking. Remove the tacking (fig 2.7).

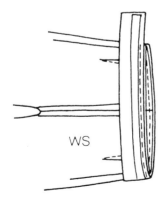

WS

Fig 2.7

> **TIP** Make it easier to turn the band over by stitching a little way from the edge of petersham, allowing 1 mm for fine fabrics, 2 mm for heavier ones.

Trim the seam allowances to 3 mm. Fold band up and press on both sides, pressing the turnings up into the band. Also press all other raw edges over on to the stiffening. This includes the two ends and sides of the extension.

Fold the band in half, either along the edge of the petersham or along the perforations in the Fold-a-Band and press, then bring the edge down on to the right side of the garment. Tuck under the raw edge so that it just covers the stitching. Pin vertically. Pin the overlap so that all edges meet. Tack all round pinned edges. Remove the pins. Press the band.

Work a row of machining all round the band with the right side uppermost. The stitching should be an even 2 mm inside the edge all round so that it catches in the petersham as well as the fabric edges. Use a straight stitch, the blind him stitch or an open embroidery stitch. Remove tackings. Press. Attach fastenings (fig 2.8).

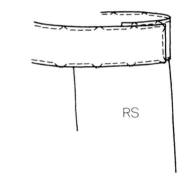

RS

Fig 2.8

Waistband with ties

Press soft Fold-a-band to the wrong side of a strip of fabric that is waist size plus enough to pass round the waist again and tie or buckle. Cut the band with a seam allowance all round beyond the Fold-a-Band. Attach the waistband to the skirt as described above but leaving two extensions at the top of the zip. Machine all round. No fastenings are needed.

WAIST OF A ONE-PIECE DRESS

If a one-piece dress is to have a belt added it helps to draw the waist in first with elastic. This gathering not only marks the waist but it holds it in position in wear so that the dress will not ride up. It also keeps the gathers evenly round the waist. The belt is worn on top.

Use a length of elastic petersham cut to fit your waist plus 2 cm. Cut a piece of fabric, on the bias if woven, 1 cm wider than the elastic and long enough to fit on the dress all round the waist.

Using a length of curved petersham fastened round your waist on top of the dress, insert pins in the dress, blousing it if you wish, level with the lower edge of the petersham. Take off the dress and check that the pins lie in an even curve. Run a row of tacking round the dress on the pins. Remove the pins.

Work zig-zag stitch along each side of the strip or casing of fabric. Turn in one end by 1 cm and place it over the centre back seam of the dress or, if there is a zip, beside it. Machine the casing to the wrong side of the dress. Have the lower edge of the casing just over the marked line and use a decorative stitch. Zig-zag stitch is satisfactory but serpentine or another open stitch looks better on the right side of the dress. On reaching the other end turn under the end of the casing to meet the first end, or beside the zip. Stitch along both sides.

Thread the elastic through the casing, overlap it by 1 cm and join by hand or machine (fig 2.9).

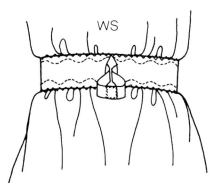

Fig 2.9

QUICK BELT

Cut a length of Fusabelta of suitable width, to the required length. The amount left for fastening will vary according to the method of fastening but if you use a buckle or a detachable clasp, as described below, add 15 cm for fastening.

Cut a length of fabric on the straight grain equal in length to the Fusabelta but 2 cm wider. Place the fabric wrong-side up on the pressing board, place the Fusabelta adhesive side down. Fold in the side of the fabric and tuck it under the backing flap. Press slowly using only the toe of the iron and making sure the fabric does not wrinkle. Turn the belt and press again.

Neaten each end of the belt by working zig-zag

stitch over the edge. Thread the ends through the clasp, attach a piece of Velcro to hold the ends back. Hem the hooked, scratchy side to the back of the belt and the soft side to the ends of the belt. This allows it to be let out if necessary. The pieces of Velcro should be 4 cm long. Use whichever width of Velcro fits the belt. Using two pieces of Velcro enables you to detach the clasp and use it on other belts (fig 2.10).

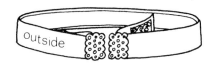

Fig 2.10

WIDE BELT

This is only satisfactory when made in firm crisp fabrics including suede and leather. Cut two pieces of fabric 8 cm wide and long enough to fit your waist plus 15 cm to fasten. Note that if using suede or leather cut only one piece and turn a single hem all round. Place the pieces of fabric right-sides together. Stitch round the outside taking 3 cm turnings, making each end narrower as shown. Slope the stitching to make the ends only 3 cm wide to prevent them from being visible when fastened. Leave a gap of 5 cm in one side. Press the stitching and turn the belt right-side out through the gap. Fold in the edges along the gap and press the belt, rolling out all the edges carefully. Either slip stitch the gap to close it or machine all round the belt on the edge.

Thread one end of the belt through a large plastic or wooden ring, fold back and hem the end. Pass the belt round your waist, thread the other end through the ring towards the inside and establish the fastening position. Sew a 4 cm length of Velcro to that end to fasten it to the back of the belt (fig 2.11).

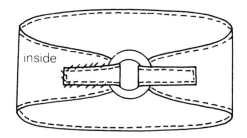

Fig 2.11

EASY FITTING BELT

Cut three long pices of fabric 2-3 cm wide. Fold in one side by 5 mm and press. Fold the other side over twice until the two folds are together. Machine down each side of the strip. Make the three pieces in the same way and press them. Put the strips side by side and machine across them 5 mm from the end. Pin this stitched end to your ironing surface and plait the strips loosely, keeping them flat. At the far end stitch across the ends to hold them together (fig 2.12). Neaten both ends with zig-zag stitch and pass through a clasp hemming the ends down firmly with the belt adjusted to fit.

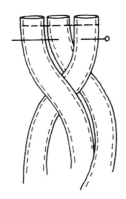

Fig 2.12

   The ease in the plait provides comfort and room for expansion.

   The ends may be held back with Velcro if the clasp is to be used on other belts.

STRAIGHT TIE BELT

Cut a length of Fold-a-Band to the length required, i.e. to pass round the waist once or twice and knot or tie in a bow. Press the Fold-a-Band to the wrong side of fabric, on the straight or on the cross. Cut out round the Fold-a-Band, allowing 3 mm seam allowance. Fold the belt right-sides together and pin with the raw edges and the pin heads to the right. Machine across the end and along the side, removing pins as you reach them, and stitching just off the edge of the Fold-a-Band. Leave a 4 cm gap in the stitching. Press the stitching (fig 2.13). Trim off the corners of the belt and turn it right-side out through the gap. Roll the edges and press carefully with the toe of the iron. Turn in the raw edges at the gap and press. Either machine all round the belt or slip stitch the folds together to close the gap.

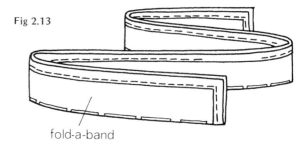

Fig 2.13

fold-a-band

QUICK SASH

This is suitable to be made in any fine fabric such as voile, chiffon and light-weight jersey.

   Cut strips of fabric on the cross 8-10 cm wide. Join the pieces to make the strip long enough to pass round your waist and tie. Leave the ends cut at an angle of $45°$. Finish the edge of the sash in one of two ways. Either use the hemming foot and roll a narrow straight or shell edge hem or set your machine to satin stitch and feed the fabric edge under the needle right-side up, turning under the edge a little and stretching it as much as possible. This produces an attractive fluted edge, more fluted on jersey than on woven fabric (fig 2.14).

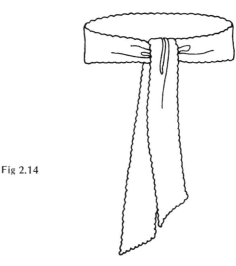

Fig 2.14

KNOTTED TUBE

Cut strips of fabric on the bias 2 cm wide, or wider if you wish, long enough to pass round your waist and tie, and also add an extra 10 cm or so for knotting. Fold the fabric right-sides together and machine 3 mm from the raw edges. Use a slight zig-zag stitch to allow the fabric to stretch and use Drima thread to ensure that the thread does not break later.

   Turn the tube right-side out. Slip a rouleau turner into the end and sew the eye to the turnings. Ease the turner through the tube and pull it out. Cut off the rouleau turner and trim the ends of the tube. Push the ends in a little way and knot them. Knot the tube at intervals all the way along, although it can be used as it is (fig 2.15).

When putting loops on the waistband of a skirt or trousers, slip the ends under the waistband before doing the final stitching. Press the loops up over the band. If you wish to stitch them down work a bar tack through the loops to hold (fig 2.17).

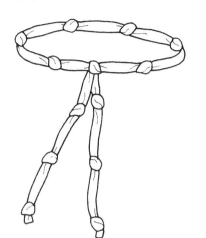

Fig 2.15

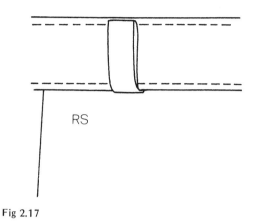

RS

Fig 2.17

> TIP If pieces of fabric have to be joined for the belt, make the joins at an angle, whether the fabric is on the cross or straight grain.

BELT LOOPS

The quickest way to make belt loops is to make a length of rouleau as described above but cutting the fabric 1 cm wide if it is light-weight.

Cut loops twice the width of the belt plus 3 mm for ease and 1 cm for the ends. Snip the stitching of the side seams or other seams, slip the ends into the seam, turn to the wrong side of the garment and re-stitch the seam to catch the loop ends (fig 2.16).

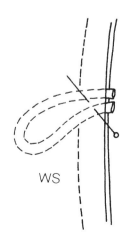

WS

Fig 2.16

3 Sleeves

Choosing styles featuring deep armholes, raglan or kimono shapes or dropped shoulder lines will make the fitting and sewing much easier. Nevertheless construction will be quicker and less liable to error if you remember the following.

RAGLAN SLEEVE

Any design with seams running from under-arm to neckline.

The raglan edges of both sleeve and bodice are on the bias and will stretch very easily. It is partly this tendency to give which makes the raglan comfortable to wear, so whilst you want to retain this property, at the same time make sure the edges are not stretched before being joined together — never lift by the top of the sleeves or bodice.

Join bodice and sleeve under-arm seams before setting sleeve to armhole. If the style shows gathers along the top of the bodice or sleeve, a dart in the top of the sleeve, or even a seam running from neck to wrist on the outside of the arm (as often found in coats), leave the process until after stitching the raglan seams.

Place right-side sleeve to right-side bodice, matching the under-arm seams. Insert one pin vertically with its head outside the edges of the fabric.

Bring neck edges of seam together so that they meet at the fitting line, not necessarily at the edge of the fabric. Pin at that point.

Tack from neck edge to under-arm and turn the work over to tack the other side from neck edge to under-arm. There is often some ease to distribute on one edge of the seam, or you may have stretched one edge inadvertently. If so, insert a few pins across the seam before tacking and take small stitches over them. If the edge is very full or badly stretched and the fabric will respond to shrinking then steam it gently after pinning, but before stitching. Remove all pins except the one at the under-arm. Machine the seam.

Alternatively the tacking may be omitted for speed, more pins inserted across the seam and the seam machined by stitching over the pins or remov-

ing them when approached. If you do not tack the seam stitch from under-arm to neck, turn work over and stitch the second section from under-arm to neck (fig 3.1).

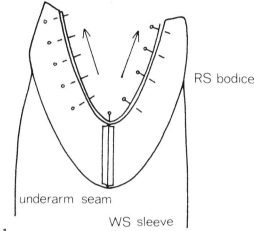

RS bodice

underarm seam

WS sleeve

Fig 3.1

TIPS Make sure pins are uppermost when machining.

Make sure pin heads are to the right and off the edge of the fabric and out of the way of the foot.

Stitch with a slight zig-zag stitch, set at about the first division on the dial, to retain the give in the seam. If you cannot zig-zag, stretch the fabric slightly.

Neaten both raw edges together after trimming. The seam should stand upright under the arm but be pressed towards the bodice along the straight sections up to the neck.

If making welt or top-stitched raglan seams, work the top stitching now.

Never snip the turnings of raglan seams; the bias property makes it quite unecessary and apart from weakening the seam, the position of the snips is visible on the outside of the garment because they cause a slight wobble or bend in the seam.

KIMONO SLEEVE

An old-fashioned term used to describe any style where the sleeve and bodice are cut in one piece.

Stitch and finish shoulder seams. The correct direction for stitching is from the neck down the outside of the arm to the wrist or hem of the sleeve. The lower part of the seam is very much on the bias, so take care not to stretch the fabric.

Some designs omit a shoulder join, cutting the sleeve and bodice pattern to a fold. This produces a very loose fit and is normally confined to casual clothes such as robes and caftans, and to short-sleeved shirts and blouses.

Join the under-arm seam by placing back and front right-sides together. Match the under-arm curve and pin. Place sleeve hems together and pin.

Tack from hem to under-arm, turn work and tack from sleeve hem to under-arm. Remove pins and machine the seam (fig 3.2).

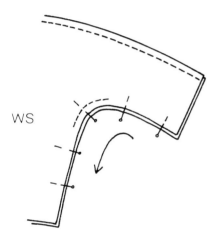

WS

Alternatively insert more pins across the seam and machine over them, omitting the tacking stage.

With both methods, stitch a second time round the pronounced curve of the under-arm, placing the second row of stitching precisely beside the first. If the fabric is loosely woven reinforce it by placing a piece of folded bias binding or a piece of folded bias fabric on the seam before working the second row of stitching.

Press the seam open, using only the toe of the iron to press round the under-arm curve.

Neaten the raw edges. Snip the seam edges three or four times round the under-arm curve at intervals of about 1.5 cm. These cut edges may have to be neatened on badly fraying fabric although there will be no strain on them apart from abrasion in wear and washing.

Occasionally kimono sleeves are cut high under the arm for a closer fit, but as this restricts movement additional room has to be provided by inserting a gusset. It may be triangular or diamond-shaped. The easiest and strongest way to attach a gusset is to turn in all edges and press.

After stitching under-arm seams place gusset wrong-side down to right-side under-arm, tack in position and machine round the outer edge with a small straight or zig-zag stitch. On the wrong side the raw edges may be neatened (fig 3.3).

Fig 3.3

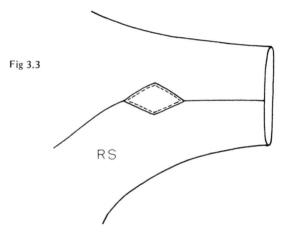

RS

TIPS When snipping turnings do not cut the bias reinforcement.

Snip at an angle to the seam — the snips are then slightly longer.

Kimono sleeves are liable to strain at the weak point under the arm so do not anchor the garment at the waist with belt loops, etc. If the garment is a dress with a waist join, make it fit loosely.

Jersey fabric will be less likely to split than woven.

DROPPED-SHOULDER SLEEVE

The main feature is a seam line below the shoulder bone and because this restricts movement the garment usually has a low armhole. The bodice has a straight or only slightly shaped armhole and the sleeve has a flattened sleeve head. Men's shirts are really drop-shouldered.

Set the sleeve to the bodice armhole before joining the side or under-arm seams. Complete any shoulder or yoke seams and then place sleeve to armhole right-sides together, matching the central sleeve-head point to the shoulder seam or a mark indicating the position of the shoulder seam. Insert a pin across the seam. Lift the fabric, hold with the sleeve uppermost and continue pinning from that point down to the under-arm (fig 3.4).

Fig 3.4

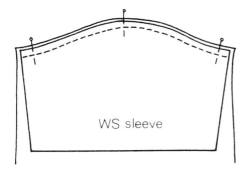

WS sleeve

Repeat on the other side of the sleeve head.

Tack, remove pins and machine, stitching with the sleeve uppermost.

Alternatively the tacking may be omitted and the seam stitched over the pins.

Press the seam towards the sleeve. Neaten raw edges or work a welt seam or machine fell seam.

Complete the sleeve and under-arm seam. Begin by pinning the under-arm seams together. Tack and stitch from there to the hemline, turn work over and stitch from under-arm seam to sleeve hem.

> **TIPS** Never snip the seam allowances. Even if the under-arm is slightly shaped there will be sufficient give for it to lie flat.
>
> Always press as for an open seam first in order to ensure a good line on the right side, even if the seam is to be completed by another method.
>
> Never insert shoulder pads. They would be placed on the natural shoulder and would therefore make it appear that you were wearing a badly fitting set-in sleeve. If the dropped-shoulder line does not look right on you, let out the garment seam allowance to its maximum, so that the seam comes further down your arm.

SET-IN SLEEVE

The seam is positioned exactly over the shoulder bone at the front, and at the back it runs in a vertical line. This sleeve must always be tacked into the armhole and fitted in order to find the correct position for the sleeve.

The sleeve head is curved in a pronounced convex shape, the armhole edge is fairly straight for about three-quarters of its length before it follows a deep concave shape for the under-arm.

There are no short cuts when making this conventional style of sleeve but I have a foolproof way of handling it so that the setting-in of the sleeve is easy.

Begin by making up the entire garment and also the sleeves. Delay the insertion of the sleeves in order to make it the final process.

With both right-sides out of garment and sleeve place the sleeve seam to the garment side seam right-sides together and pin.

The two raw edges are similar in shape and will fit together easily so, without stretching, hold the under-arm sections of the sleeve and garment together and tack. The amount that can be tacked at this stage will be about 8 cm on each side of the seam. Fasten off the tacking (fig 3.5).

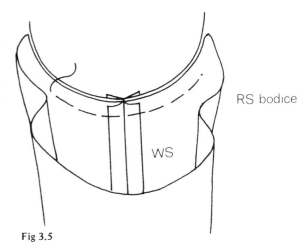

RS bodice

WS

Fig 3.5

The shape of the sleeve head is so different from that of the top of the armhole that it should be held carefully. The sleeve is bigger than the armhole to provide room for movement and this excess fabric in the sleeve must be controlled.

Put your hand inside the garment and take hold of the sleeve head and the top of the garment armhole, at the shoulder seam. Holding the two together, pull them through the neckline and then flip them both over so that the sleeve is lying on top of the armhole but the edges are still together. Do not pull the whole of the sleeve through and do not turn the garment inside out; rather use the remainder of the garment as a cushion with which to support the sleeve.

Put the central sleeve-head point to the shoulder seam (or shoulder point if there is no seam). Insert one pin across the seam. Move your hand to support one side of the sleeve head between this pin and the end of the tacking. Spread out your fingers under the two edges and pin. Start by inserting one pin in the centre of the area, then pin in the middle of each smaller area and so on. Continue putting in pins to divide up the ease into smaller and smaller bulges. Any large amount of ease left undivided will form a pleat when stitched (fig 3.6).

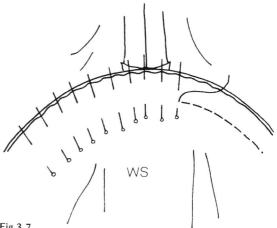

Fig 3.7

garment, remove the tacking from the sleeve head only, trim the surplus fabric from the armhole in a smooth line, leaving 1.5 cm seam allowance.

Re-pin the sleeve head, tack and try on again.

Stitch the sleeves into the armholes. Use a medium-size stitch, work with sleeve uppermost and machine very slowly beside the tacking stitches. If any part of the sleeve head begins to form a wrinkle, stop, use a pin to flatten it or snip the next tacking stitch and proceed.

Remove tackings and trim the turnings to 1 cm before neatening them together.

Press from the right side with the turnings facing towards the sleeve to support the sleeve head.

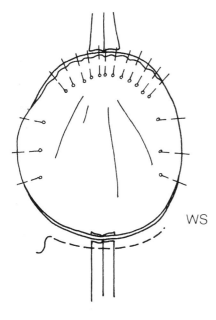

Fig 3.6

Move to the other side of the sleeve head and pin in the same way.

When distributing this ease remember that the most should go to the front of the shoulder seam to provide room for the shoulder bone that protrudes. There should be a little ease over the top and to the back of the shoulder seam but none down the straight part of the back armhole because most people are almost hollow at that point.

Turn garment so that sleeve is right-side out and see how it hangs. Adjust pins if you can detect any obvious bulges of fullness.

Tack the sleeve head with small stitches. Insert the needle under a pin, remove the pin and complete the stitch, insert the needle under the next pin and so on. This ensures that the ease stays put. Fasten off the tacking (fig 3.7).

Try on the garment. If the shoulder seam is too long and the sleeve needs lifting, mark a new line while it is on you, with tailor's chalk. Take off the

TIPS Never use a gathering thread in a plain sleeve; it makes it impossible to achieve a smooth sleeve head.

Never cut off the sleeve head if it seems too full; persevere. It is only correct manipulation which is required.

If you have sloping shoulders and always have difficulty in avoiding a droopy look, pop shoulder pads in to support the sleeves.

If you are putting a zip in the side seam, stitch the seam to the point at the base of the zip position, leaving it open at the shoulder end. Put in the zip with the slider at the seam allowance level. Work a bar tack to hold together the folded edges at the top of the zip and set in the sleeve, stitching above the zip (fig 3.8).

When making puff sleeves insert a gathering thread over the sleeve head but hold the sleeve and manipulate it in the same way as described for a plain sleeve.

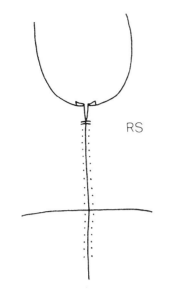

RS

Fig 3.8

SHORT SLEEVES

Machined hem

This is quicker than hand sewing but in addition it is stronger. It is important to avoid the impression that you machined the sleeve hem in order to save time by working two rows of stitching, one at the hem edge and one at the sleeve edge. You can therefore make it look attractive if the stitch is zig-zag or a decorative machine stitch.

It is further improved if you lengthen the sleeve when cutting out in order to allow for a finished hem of at least 3 cm.

If the fabric is reversible, e.g. plain polyester/cotton, work machine fell seams on the garment and turn the hem over to the right side to finish it, giving a cuff effect (fig 3.9).

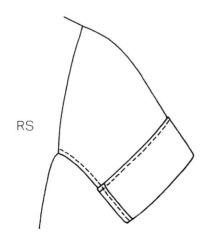

RS

Fig 3.9

> **TIP** Begin and end machine stitching at the under-arm seam.

Wundaweb hem

Allow for a hem exactly 3 cm in depth, adding extra when cutting out or shortening the sleeve if necessary. After stitching the seam, neaten the raw edge at the bottom of the sleeve.

Turn it up to the right side to exactly 3 cm and press the folded edge. This is best done by sliding the sleeve on to the sleeve board and holding an adjustable marker set to the correct measurement, while pressing and moving the sleeve round.

Cut a length of Wundaweb long enough to go round the sleeve plus 1 cm overlap. Slip this under the hem edge, making sure the edge of the Wundaweb strip is exactly in the fold. Overlap the ends. Make sure the Wundaweb is hidden, then pull the sleeve outwards, holding fabric only. This avoids tightening of the hem by the adhesive.

Press the hem using a hot iron and damp cloth. Press only the depth of the hem, not over the neatened edge. Press several times in each place to ensure that the adhesive has completely melted.

> **TIPS** Use the iron sideways, i.e. parallel with the hem edge, to avoid pressing over the neatened edge.
>
> Do not turn a deep hem on fine fabric such as voile, and do not use Wundaweb on fine fabric.

Turn-back cuff

Add a cuff or replace a separate cuff as follows. When cutting out extend the length of the sleeve so that it measures 28 cm from under-arm to hem. Straighten the sleeve seam edges if they slope inwards.

Stitch sleeve seam and neaten lower edge of sleeve. Fold hem 10 cm deep to wrong side of sleeve and press. Place a length of Fold-a-Band on the wrong side with the central holes exactly over the pressed crease. Press in position. Re-fold the sleeve hem.

Fold sleeve hem over to the right side to form a cuff, turning up 5.5 cm and pressing. Insert a few pins vertically to hold it back.

Turn sleeve wrong-side out. Slip a length of Wundaweb under the neatened edge of the hem. Make sure it is completely concealed. Press once only, using a hot iron and damp cloth (fig 3.10).

Fig 3.10

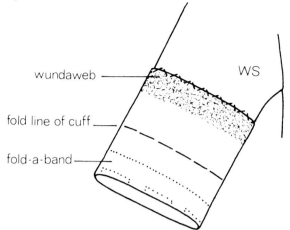

wundaweb

WS

fold line of cuff

fold-a-band

Fig 3.11

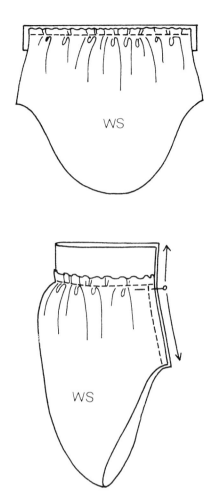

WS

WS

Remove the pins and unfold the cuff. Press the hem containing the Wundaweb until the adhesive has completely melted. Where the hem crosses the under-arm, work a few herringbone stitches.

Fold the cuff back into position and press.

TIPS Position the join of the Fold-a-Band at the under-arm seam.

If the fabric is soft or floppy, work a bar tack between the cuff and the sleeve at the under-arm seam.

Gathered into band

Check that the band is the correct length to fit the top of the arm. Attach interfacing to wrong side if needed.

Insert gathering thread along lower edge of sleeve, starting and finishing 3 cm from the sleeve edge.

Fold the band and the sleeve to find the centre and mark each with tailor's chalk.

Place the band to the sleeve, right-sides together and edges together. Match the centre points and pin. Bring each end of the band to the edge of the sleeve and pin. Pull up the gathering thread and wind the end round a pin. Distribute the gathers so that rather more of the ease appears at the centre of the sleeve and less at the ends near the under-arm. Pin all the way along and tack. Remove pins (fig 3.11).

Machine with gathers uppermost. Remove tacking thread and gathering thread. Trim the raw edges to 3 mm wide. Turn sleeve right-side up and press so that the turnings lie towards the band. Press only the band, do not flatten the gathers.

Fold sleeve right-sides together, pin across the

Fig 3.12

seam where the band joins the sleeve, keeping turnings in position. Machine from the band join to the under-arm, remove the pin, turn the sleeve over and machine across the band. Press the seam open and neaten the raw edges (fig 3.12).

Trim down the turnings within the band to 3 mm.

With the sleeve right-side out, fold the band over and crease, insert a couple of pins and press the fold carefully.

Turn sleeve wrong-side out. Turn under the raw edge, bringing the fold down on to the machine stitching. Tack and remove pins.

Complete the band either by hemming by hand, working a stitch in each machine stitch, or if you prefer to machine it, bring the fold down further to cover the machining, tack and stitch from the right side. Use a straight stitch or a small zig-zag or, if suitable, machine embroidery stitch. Two rows can be worked, one on each edge of the sleeve band (fig 3.13).

Fig 3.13

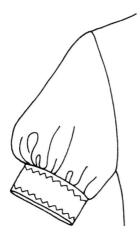

Cut out sleeves twice in fabric, or once in fabric and once in lining material. Allow only 1 cm hem along the lower edges, not the hem allowed on the pattern. Place them right sides together in pairs, each sleeve against its under sleeve.

Machine along the lower edge, taking 1 cm turning. Press the join open.

Fold sleeves right-sides together, matching under-arm seam edges. Insert one pin across the seam with pin head extending beyond the raw edges of the fabric (fig 3.14).

Machine the under-arm seam, taking 1.5 cm or whatever seam allowance there is. Start just before the pin and stitch to the end. Remove the pin, turn the sleeve over and machine from the seam to the raw edges.

Trim the seam edges to 1 cm; snip turnings above and below the join. Press the seam open.

With sleeve wrong-side outwards, roll the lining or inner sleeve over the outer one so that it is on the outside. Hold the lower edge of the sleeve, roll the inner sleeve towards you to reveal 1 mm or so of outer sleeve. Slide it on to the sleeve board and press, revolving the sleeve in order to press all round (fig 3.15).

> **TIP** Cut the sleeve band to take Fold-a-Band and the central fold position is easy to find.

Double sleeve

A plain short sleeve can be made more quickly from two layers of fabric. In addition it is easier and firmer to handle, and, subsequently, creases less in wear and in washing. If the fabric is medium- to heavy-weight or thick, use lining fabric, cotton or polyester and cotton lawn, or nylon jersey.

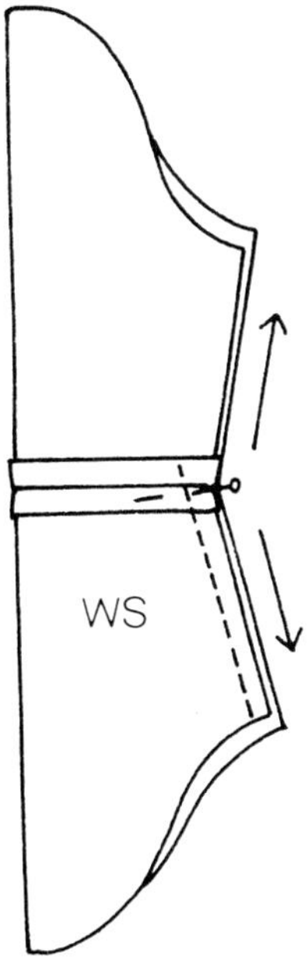

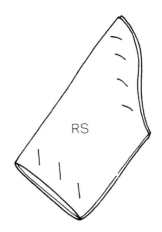

Fig 3.15

Turn sleeve right-side out and baste round the lower edge. Baste round sleeve head to hold the two layers together.

Set the sleeve in as one layer.

WS

Fig 3.14

TIPS When making a lined garment make the sleeves like this but set in only the outer sleeve, using the edge of the lining to neaten the arm-hole join.

If the lining is not a good match prevent any possibility of it showing in wear by working a row of machining round the lower edge of the sleeve a little way from the edge in order to make sleeve look decorative.

This method can also be used for long sleeves that are full at the wrist. Contrasting colours can be used with effect especially for evening wear in light-weight fabrics. Do not line long-fitted sleeves in this way because it is not possible to allow the ease needed in the lining.

LONG SLEEVES

Some of these finishes are also suitable for full short sleeves

Gathered at wrist

Elastic

Stitch the sleeve seam. Make sure the sleeve is the correct length, allowing 5 mm for a hem to take elastic 3 mm wide.

Neaten the raw edge and turn it up 1 cm. Press all round. Machine on the folded edge from the right side with a small zig-zag or decorative stitch. Note that the width of the stitch should be no more than 2 on the machine dial.

Turn sleeve wrong-side out and insert pins at intervals across the hem to hold it up. Using the same machine stitch as before, work round the sleeve just below the neatened edge. Fasten off the end of the machining leaving a 5 mm gap in the stitching.

Measure elastic round your wrist and cut, allowing 1 cm for joining. Thread through the sleeve, join by oversewing firmly (fig 3.16).

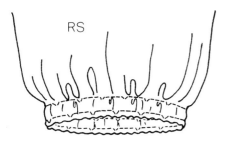

Fig 3.16

An alternative method is to use shirring elastic on the machine spool for stitching the hem instead of inserting elastic later. A third row of shirring may be needed between the two rows to ensure sufficient grip.

Elastic with frilled edge

Cut out the sleeves sufficiently long to allow for the frilled edge plus 1 cm for the hem. Depending on the fabric, allow between 2 and 3 cm for the frill but no more than 4 cm or it will extend beyond the thumb joint.

Stitch the sleeve seam. Turn a narrow hem round the lower edge and machine with a straight, zig-zag or embroidery stitch.

With sleeve wrong-side out measure the frill depth from the hem and mark round with tailor's chalk.

Cut strips of fabric on the cross 1.5 cm wide, to take elastic 8 mm wide. Work a small zig-zag stitch along each side. Place strip wrong-side down to wrong side sleeve with one edge on the chalk mark. Tack down the centre to attach it to the sleeve. Leave a slit for inserting the elastic by turning in both ends of the strip so that the folded edges meet. Press. Machine along each edge of the strip with a small zig-zag or embroidery stitch (fig 3.17).

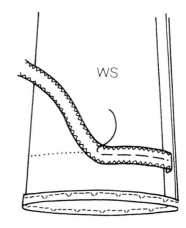

WS

Fig 3.17

Measure elastic round your wrist and cut, allowing 1 cm to join. Thread through slot and join by over-sewing firmly.

Alternatively put shirring elastic on the machine spool and work three or five rows of shirring round the sleeve. Begin by marking up a chalk line on the right side of the sleeve and work the stitching from that side. On completing one circuit do not end the stitching but lift the machine foot and move the work slightly to one side (the width of one prong of the foot), lower the foot and work the next row.

Instead of shirring elastic use narrow conventional elastic cut to fit your wrist plus 1 cm to overlap. Mark the position with tailor's chalk on the wrong side of the sleeve. Set your machine to a medium width zig-zag (about Mark 2½ on the dial). Slip the elastic over the wrong side of the sleeve and put under the machine foot, anchor the elastic by reversing for a couple of stitches, then stitch forward but stretch the elastic as much as possible as you stitch. Obviously you must use up all the fabric as you machine. If you have not operated this particular technique before, it helps to practise to see just how much you can stretch the elastic (fig 3.18).

It also helps to use soft elastic (which is made from a single flat strip of latex covered with viscose yarn) because it stretches more than elastic made of several cores.

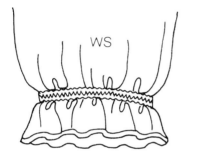

Fig 3.18

If the lower edge of sleeve is straight or almost straight, the frilled edge can be double. Cut the sleeves long enough to allow twice the frill depth in addition to the basic length plus 3 cm for the elastic. After stitching the sleeve seam neaten the lower raw edge. Turn up and press a fold to form the lower edge of the frill. Work a row of basting round the sleeve above this fold to hold the surplus fabric in position. With sleeve wrong-side up work two rows of small-size zig-zag stitch, one just inside the neatened raw edge, the other 1 cm away. Leave a gap in one of them and thread elastic through (fig 3.19).

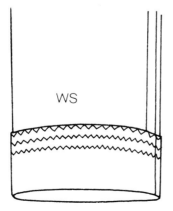

Fig 3.19

Prepare the sleeve as above but work rows of shirring instead of inserting conventional elastic. Work from the right side, having put a guide line in tailor's chalk for the first row. As the fabric is double you may need six or seven rows of shirring to obtain sufficient grip.

Band with frill

Cut the sleeves to the exact length plus enough to allow for a frilled edge, but do not plan for a deep frill. Cut two strips of fabric 4 cm wide. The strip should be long enough to pass over your hand plus 3 cm for seam allowance. Turn in and press a 1 cm turning along each side. Insert a gathering thread across the sleeve at frill depth. Mark the centre of the sleeve and band (fig 3.20).

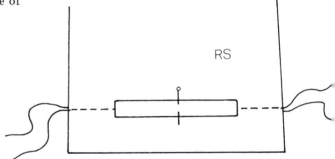

Fig 3.20

Place wrong-side band to right-side sleeve, matching centre marks and pinning the ends of the strips to the sleeve edges.

Pull up the gathering thread, even out the gathers but avoid having any within 2 cm of the sides of the sleeves. Tack the strip to the sleeve. Attach the strip to the sleeve by working a straight or zig-zag stitch along each edge.

Remove tacking. Fold sleeve right-sides together and stitch the seam. Turn up a narrow hem round the lower edge of the sleeve (fig 3.21).

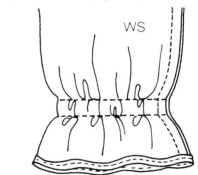

Fig 3.21

The above method gives a loose fit at the wrist. For a tighter fit cut the bands to fit your wrist, allowing 3 cm for turning in the ends.

Stitch the sleeve seam, leaving 6 cm open at the wrist. Neaten the seam and press open. Turn up a narrow hem round the bottom of the sleeve, stitch by hand or machine.

Turn in and press 1 cm along each side of the band. Insert a gathering thread in the sleeve. Place the strip wrong-side down to right-side sleeve, matching centres. Turn in ends of band and pin beside the opening. Pull up the gathers evenly across the sleeve. Tack the band to the sleeve, tacking across the ends as well as along the sides. Machine all round the band with a straight or zig-zag machine stitch.

Fasten the wrist opening by making a worked loop on the band at the front of the sleeve and sew a button to the back. When fastened, the band should meet edge to edge (fig 3.22).

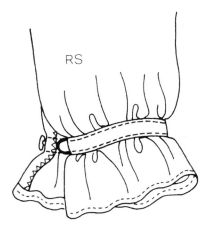

Fig 3.22

TIPS Sleeves with elastic in the wrist will ride up unless additional length is allowed. Cut sleeves at least 6 cm longer than required; they look nicer anyway if puffed up a little.

Begin and end bands, crossway strips, elastic, etc., at the under-arm seam so that joins are not visible.

Elastic seems to become tighter as the day wears on so to avoid this make sure it is long enough. Pin it round your wrist and wear it for ten minutes or so before cutting it to size.

It is essential to use synthetic thread, e.g. Drima, with elastic and shirring elastic since cotton thread may break under the strain.

With cuffs

Jersey cuff

The cuff can be either made from fabric or you can use cuff ribbing, or you can knit your own ribbing. Ribbing that you buy may be tubular.

If you knit your own, knit it the required depth and sew it up, making sure it will slip over your hand.

To make fabric cuffs, cut strips of jersey fabric across the width of the fabric to provide maximum stretch. The width should be at least 9 cm for a narrow cuff, allowing 1 cm on each edge for attaching to the sleeve. The cuff should be long enough to slip over your hand when joined. Make it fairly tight. Join the cuff with a slight zig-zag stitch. Trim the edges and press open, or, if the fabric curls up, press to one side (fig 3.23).

Fig 3.23

Fold the cuff with wrong-sides together and press. Note that fabric cuffs and purchased ribbing are folded double to attach, but hand-knitted ones should be single in order to avoid excessive bulk.

Join the sleeve seam and neaten. Insert a gathering thread round the lower edge of the sleeve. Slip the sleeve, wrong-side out, over the cuff. Pin at four equidistant points. Seams must be together. Pull up the gathering thread until the sleeve fits the cuff, *when the cuff is extended to its maximum size by stretching.* Insert additional pins with the pin heads extending beyond the raw edge of the fabric. Slip this assembly over the free arm of your machine or, if you have a flat-bed model, turn so that it is cuff-side out-wards and slide it under the machine foot. Attach sleeve to cuff with a zig-zag stitch set at No. 1 on the dial. As you sew, stretch the cuff as much as possible, removing the pins as you come to them. Remove the gathering thread. Trim the raw edges to 5 mm and neaten all together with a zig-zag stitch (figs 3.24 and 3.25).

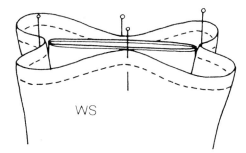

Fig 3.24

Fig 3.25

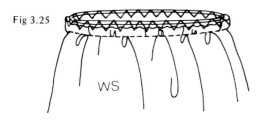

Wrap cuff

Use this method with lightweight woven fabrics (fig 3.26).

Use the cuff pattern provided in your pattern and cut out and attach the interfacing. Alternatively if you have no pattern, cut strips of Fold-a-Band adhesive-side down to wrong-side fabric with central holes exactly on the straight grain. Press to adhere. Cut out allowing 1 cm seam allowance all round the outer edge of the Fold-a-Band.

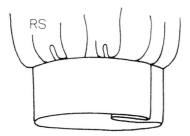

Fig 3.26

Fold cuff right-sides together and machine across the end to join, taking 1 cm turning. Press open and trim the edges down to 5 mm. Stitch and neaten the sleeve seam. Insert a gathering thread across the lower edge.

Hold cuff right-side outwards and slip the sleeve over it with right side against the cuff. Pin the seams together and pin at three other points, spacing the pins out equally. Pull up the gathering thread until the sleeve fits the cuff. Wind the end of the thread round a pin and distribute the gathers at a point 2 cm from the seam, towards the back of the sleeve so that it is free from gathers. This is where the cuff will wrap. Tack the sleeve to the cuff.

Machine round the sleeve with gathers uppermost. Remove tackings and gathering thread and trim the turnings down to 5 mm. Turn sleeve right-side out and press the join so that the turnings lie towards the cuff. Do not press over the gathers.

Turn the sleeve wrong-side out, fold the cuff over in half (Fold-a-Band will automatically crease at the centre) and press the crease. Turn under the raw

edge of the cuff to fall on the machine stitching. Insert pins vertically and hem into the machine stitches, or tack the fold to cover the machining completely and machine the cuff from the right side, just below the join. If you do this, work a matching row of machining near the lower edge (fig 3.27).

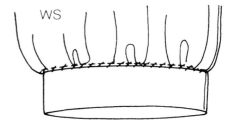

Fig 3.27

Put the sleeve on, wrap the cuff over to fit, where the flat area comes, and mark the size of the wrap with pins. Take off the sleeve.

Attach fastenings. Choose between hemming a narrow strip of Velcro in position and attaching two press studs. When fastened, the cuff must fit the wrist comfortably. For decoration, buttons may be sewn on the outside (fig 3.28).

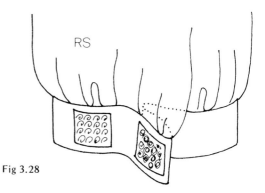

Fig 3.28

With opening and cuff

The position of a sleeve opening is marked on the pattern. If you wish to make the opening in that position mark that position on the fabric and cut.

With wrong side towards you roll a tiny hem along the cut edges, hemming by hand as you roll it. Half way along, stop and make a small horizontal snip at the top of the cut, making a snip on each side of the cut. This enables you to roll the hem evenly to the top. Hem the second side. Press. Fold the sleeve with right sides together and pin to hold the rolled edges of the opening together. Pin at the top of the opening and 3 cm beyond it. Place under the machine and stitch from the top of the opening, level with the edge of the rolled hem, to the folded edge, stopping just below the pin at the 3 cm point. The stitching should slope gradually as for a dart (fig 3.29).

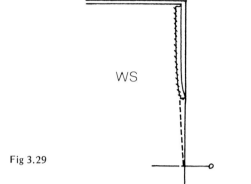

Fig 3.29

Press this little dart flat so that the fabric lies equally on each side of the opening. Finish by working herringbone stitch over the raw edge and make a bar tack to hold the two hemmed edges together at the top. Stitch the sleeve seam.

Alternatively the opening in the sleeve can be left in the under-arm seam and the cuff fastened at that position with one button and buttonhole or a press stud.

Stitch the sleeve seam, leaving 7 cm open at the wrist. Press the seam open and neaten the edges. Cut strips of Wundaweb 8 cm long and 1 cm wide, slip them under the neatened edges beside the slit and press well with a hot iron and a damp cloth (fig 3.30).

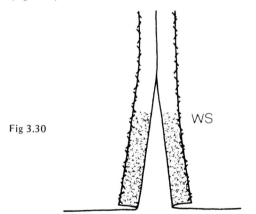

Fig 3.30

Make the cuff for both types of opening by cutting out in fabric, using the pattern provided and attach interfacing, or if you have no pattern, press strips of Fold-a-Band on to the wrong side of your fabric and cut out allowing 1 cm turning round the outer edge. The cuff should be 21 cm long without turnings, or, your wrist measurement plus 5 cm ease and 2-5 cm overlap plus turnings.

Fold cuff wrong-sides together and machine across the ends. Trim edges and corners. Turn cuff right-side out and press (fig 3.31). If you wish to top stitch the ends and lower edge do it now.

Fig 3.31

Baste along the cuff to hold the two layers together.

Place cuff to right-side sleeve with ends of the cuff level with the edges of the opening. Pin. Pull up gathers or insert tucks if it is a shirt-style sleeve. Tack cuff to sleeve and machine. Remove tacking stitches and gathering thread. Trim raw edges to 5 mm and neaten all together with zig-zag stitch. Press the turnings down towards the cuff (fig 3.32).

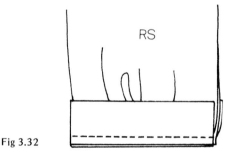

Fig 3.32

Attach fastenings so that the cuff overlaps to fit when fastened. Use a button and buttonhole, a narrow strip of Velcro, button snaps, metal studs or press studs.

> **TIP** If it worries you that the join might show at the end of the cuff, make a corner at the buttonhole end when you first stitch the ends. Turn cuff right-side out including the corner, snip the turnings at the end of the machine stitching and attach the cuff as described but making sure this overlap corner is located at the front of the sleeve (fig 3.33).
>
> For a quick sleeve opening, measure about a quarter of the way along the wrist edge of the sleeve, on the back of the sleeve, and make two snips in the edge 1-1½ cm apart. Cut a small piece of Wundaweb and press back the fabric with it underneath. Make and attach the cuff (fig 3.34).

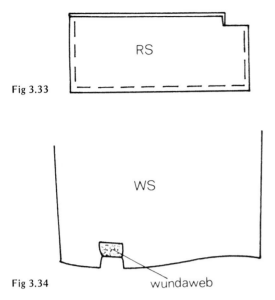

Fig 3.33

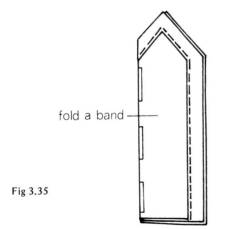

Fig 3.34   wundaweb

With strap

A long sleeve of normal width can be decorated and also reduced in width by a strap.

Cut two pieces of Fold-a-Band 20 cm long and trim one end of each to a point. Press these to the wrong side of a piece of fabric. Cut out round the outside, leaving 1 cm seam allowances. Fold straps right-sides together, pin, and machine round the point and down the long side, just off the edge of the interfacing (fig 3.35). Trim the turnings. Cut off the point. Using a rouleau turner, turn straps right-side out. Roll the edges and press.

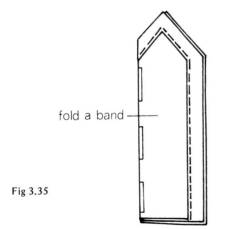

fold a band

Fig 3.35

Place straps against the back edge of the sleeve 10 cm above the hemline on the right side. The strap must extend across the sleeve. Hold it in place with a piece of Sellotape. Fold sleeve right-sides together and machine the seam. Press it open and neaten the edges including the edges of the straps. Turn sleeve

right-side out and press strap towards the front of the sleeve (fig 3.36).

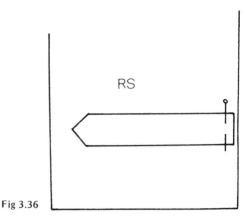

Fig 3.36

Turn up the sleeve hems. Bring straps across sleeves, gathering the sleeve a little and sew a button through the point of the strap and the sleeve (fig 3.37).

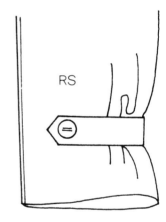

Fig 3.37

An alternative sleeve strap can be made by making two straps 30 cm long for each sleeve. Place one on each edge of the sleeve and anchor. Stitch the seam, turn up the hem. Bring the straps over the sleeve and tie (fig 3.38).

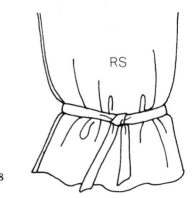

Fig 3.38

4 Necklines and collars

NECKLINES

Necklines may be faced or bound, as described in the chapters containing those processes, but they have to have an opening as well which may contain a zip.

Bound and tied

Round necklines may be finished with a narrow binding as described in chapter 10 *Edges and hems*. The garment is often gathered into the binding. The ties may be made by leaving long extensions of cross-way fabric to be machined or hemmed when the neck binding is finished. Alternatively ties of ribbon, cord or crochet may be inserted into the ends of the neckline binding (fig 4.1).

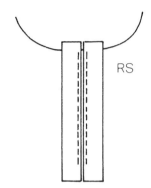

Fig 4.2

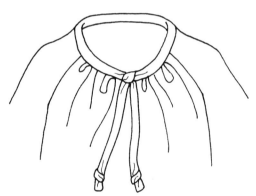

Fig 4.1

> TIP Thread beads on to the ends of the ties; sew in place or tie a knot in the tie.

The slit opening below the ties may be made in one of the following ways.

Straight bound opening

Chalk a line on the right side of the garment to indicate the position of the opening.

Cut two crossway strips of fabric the length of this line plus 1 cm, and 2 cm wide. Place the strips on the right side of the garment, right-side down with the raw edges meeting on the chalk line. Pin (fig 4.2).

Machine 3 mm from each raw edge, fastening off each row of stitching at the base. The two rows must be parallel and the same length.

Turn the work over and cut the garment fabric between the rows of stitching. Snip to within 1 cm of the bottom before cutting out at an angle to the ends of the two rows of stitching (fig 4.3).

Use the toe of the iron to press over the strips.

Fold the raw edge of each strip over twice, bringing the fold to cover the machine stitches. Tack and press.

Turn the work over and machine from the right side, stitching exactly in the dent formed

Fig 4.3

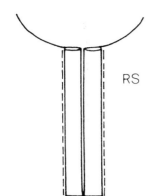

Fig 4.4

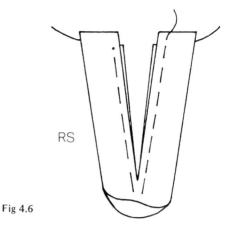

Fig 4.6

by the strip. Fasten off at the lower end (fig 4.4).

Fold the bindings down on to the lower part of the garment so that the triangle cut earlier stands upright. Insert a pin across the bindings to hold them together and machine across the base of the triangle, attaching the strips (fig 4.5).

Fold the opening back and press.

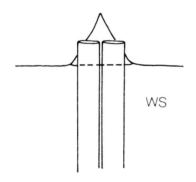

Fig 4.5

Use the toe of the iron to press the strip outwards. Fold its raw edge over twice so that it covers the machine stitches. Pin across the strip and tack. Remove the pins. Turn the work right-side up and machine in the well which is formed by the strip or hem on the wrong side (figs 4.7 and 4.8).

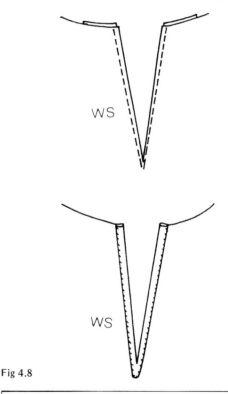

Fig 4.8

> **TIP** If the fabric frays easily press a small square of Bondaweb to the wrong side of the garment at the end of the chalk line, before you start.

V bound opening

Mark the length of the opening on the right side of the garment. Cut a crossway strip of fabric 2 cm wide and twice the length of the opening.

Cut the opening, cutting a V 2 cm wide at the top. Place the strip right-side down to the right side of the garment and pin. Have the raw edges level at the top of the V but gradually reduce the turning taken on the garment until, at the base of the V, you take only a couple of threads. Tack, then turn the work over so that the garment is uppermost and machine. It helps to open out the V as straight as possible. Take a 3 cm turning all the way along the crossway strip (fig 4.6).

> **TIPS** If the fabric frays easily press a small square of Bondaweb to the wrong side of the fabric at the base of the marked opening, before cutting it.
>
> Use a small machine stitch to attach the crossway strip, especially at the base of the V.

Strap opening

For speed and accuracy use soft Fold-a-Band inside
the strap. It serves as an interfacing as well as being
a guide to stitching straight. Adapt the strap width
indicated on the pattern to the width of the Fold-
a-Band.

Mark the position and length of the opening on
the right side with chalk.

On the wrong side press a small rectangle of
Bondaweb to cover the bottom of the opening.
Peel off the paper (fig 4.9).

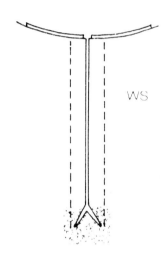

Fig 4.10

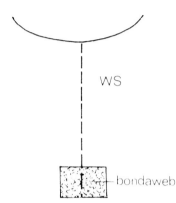

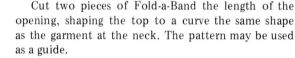

Fig 4.9

Cut two pieces of Fold-a-Band the length of the
opening, shaping the top to a curve the same shape
as the garment at the neck. The pattern may be used
as a guide.

Press the strips on to the wrong side of fabric
with one edge exactly on the straight grain. Cut out
round the Fold-a-Band, leaving 1.5 cm seam allowance all round.

Place the strips right-side down to the right side
of the garment with the two raw edges meeting close
together over the chalk mark. Tack the strips down.
Machine, using the edge of the Fold-a-Band as a guide.
Start at the bottom on each side, working to the neck
edge each time to make two parallel rows of stitching
equal in length (fig 4.10).

Trim the band edge down to 3 mm.

Turn the garment over and cut between the rows
of stitching to within 3 cm of the bottom. From
there cut out at an angle to the ends of the stitching (fig 4.11).

Using the toe of the iron press the bands over.

Finish the band on the right-hand side by turning
it up across the bottom, fold it on the centre of the
Fold-a-Band and tack. Turn under the raw edge of
the band and tack. Hem down the fold and slip
stitch across the bottom, or machine all round close
to the edge (fig 4.12).

Fig 4.11

Fig 4.12

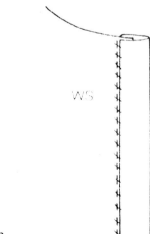

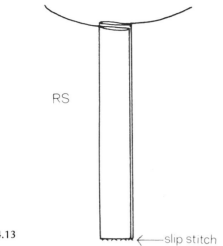

Fig 4.13

Work any buttonholes now.

Pin the band in position over the triangle of fabric at the base of the opening and slip stitch it in place by hand (fig. 4.13).

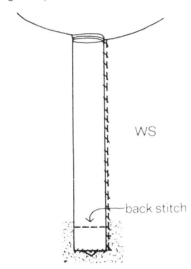

Fig 4.14

Complete the left band by hemming down the length. At the base trim the raw edges down to 3 mm, neaten and hold in place under the other band with a few back stitches (fig 4.14).

> **TIPS** If the pattern provides a piece that combines the strap with a neck facing, still use Fold-a-Band, attaching it to the wrong side of the facing at the centre-front edge.
>
> Even it the garment has a strap opening that extends to the hemline, still use Fold-a-Band, both as a guide and as an interfacing.

Seam opening

If there is a seam consider putting the opening in it. Construct an open seam, leaving the top unstitched, neaten the edges and hold the turnings back with a very narrow strip of Wundaweb. Allow the Wundaweb to extend beyond the base of the slit of the opening (fig 4.15).

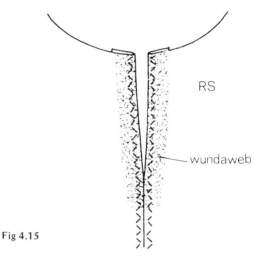

Fig 4.15

Work a straight, zig-zag or decorative stitch down each edge between 3 and 5 mm from the edge. The stitching may be continued down beside the actual seam too.

Faced opening

A method of making a slit opening where there is no seam. It is more often used in wrists of long sleeves rather than in an obvious position such as the centre front, although it could be used at the centre back of a neckline. Do not use on transparent fabrics as the facings will show.

The opening has a weak spot at the base but this can be strengthened if the opening is made as follows.

Decide on how long the opening needs to be without strain when putting on the garment and mark the line with chalk on the wrong side. Cut a rectangle of fabric on the straight grain 5 cm wide and 3 cm longer than the opening. Press a strip of Bondaweb down the centre 4 cm wide and peel off the paper backing. If the fabric frays neaten the two long edges and one of the shorter ones.

Place the rectangle right-side down to the right side of the garment with the centre over the line of the opening. Attach with a couple of pins (fig 4.16).

With the garment wrong-side up machine 2-3 mm beside the chalk line, work to a point at the base and stitch up the other side 2-3 mm from the chalk.

Cut between the two rows and snip right into

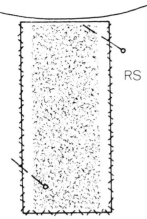

Fig 4.16

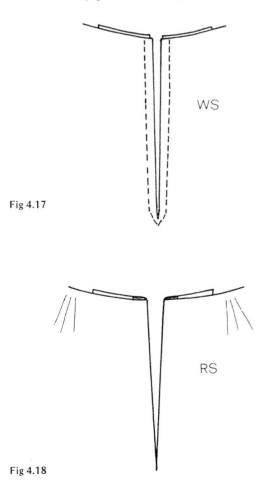

Fig 4.17

Fig 4.18

the point. Roll the facing completely to the wrong side, press the edge with your fingers, tack if the fabric is springy, then press from the right side. The Bondaweb will not only hold the rectangle in place during wear but will help prevent fraying at the weak base (figs 4.17 and 4.18).

COLLARS

Collars are made from double fabric; the ones that are quickest to cut and construct are those made from a piece of fabric that is folded.

Most collars need some interfacing in them.

The conventional methods of attaching are time-consuming, so short cuts can be taken in joining the collar to the neckline, employing methods that are often used in ready-made clothes.

Even though these ways of attaching are quick to do there are several points to remember in order to ensure good results.

Trim down the seam allowance on the neckline of the garment to 1 cm. This makes it easier to handle.

Mark the centre back and centre front of the neckline — one may be marked already by a zip or other opening.

Pin the collar to the neckline, inserting the pins across the seam, matching centre back and centre front points.

If there is any ease in the collar it should be arranged approximately where the shoulder seams fall.

Bias roll

The collar is a rectangle of fabric cut on the cross, the exact length of the garment's neckline and four times as wide as the finished effect. It is usually fastened at the back above a zip.

Cut a strip of light or soft iron-on Vilene and press it to one edge of the collar. The Vilene should be less than a quarter of the width of the rectangle (fig 4.19).

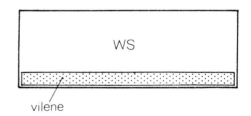

vilene

Fig 4.19

On the garment, fold back the centre front or back seam allowance or facing on to the right side and pin. Fold the collar wrong-side together and machine across the ends. Trim the turnings and turn the corners right-side out. Press. Fold the collar and press a crease to mark the centre front. Place collar to neck edge with the interfaced edge against the garment. Pin the centre front; pin the ends of the collar at the centre back on top of the turned-back facing. Pin at intervals in between. Tack and machine from end to end. Trim the turnings to 5 mm and zig-zag to neaten. Press the seam down into the garment and the collar up, fold the facings to the wrong side. Press. Allow the collar to roll over (figs 4.20, 4.21 and 4.22).

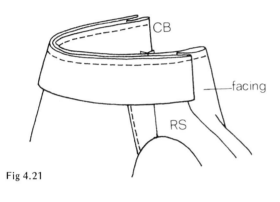

Fig 4.20

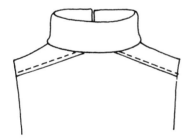

Fig 4.21

Fig 4.22

Bias finish and tie

The collar is a long piece of bias fabric that fits the neck edge of the garment but with ends long enough to tie at the front. The width can be twice the finished collar width or if you want it to roll, four times the width. Pieces of fabric may have to be joined to make a piece long enough. Make sure the join falls at the centre back.

Measure the length of the neck edge of the garment, cut a piece of iron-on Vilene to the same length and 1 cm less in width than the stand of the collar. Press it to one edge of the bias fabric, in the centre (fig 4.23).

Fig 4.23

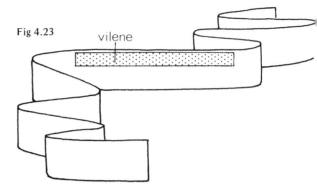

On the garment, fold the front facing on to the right side and pin. Measure the distance from the fold at the edge back to the centre front — usually 1-2 cm, depending on the width of the facing. Fold the bias piece with right sides together and machine across each end and along the edge, leaving a gap in the middle equal to the size of the neckline on the garment, minus the distance measured across the facing (fig 4.24).

Fig 4.24

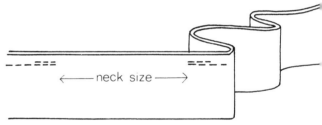

Trim the turnings and turn the tie ends right-side out and press. Snip the turnings at the ends of the stitching. Match the centre back to the centre back of the garment and pin.

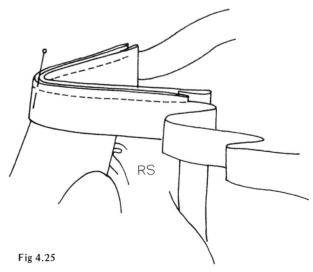

Fig 4.25

Bring the ends of the neck section to the centre front on top of the facing and pin. Pin at intervals. Tack and machine from end to end (fig 4.25). Trim the turnings to 5 mm and zig-zag to neaten. Fold the facings on to the wrong side. Press the neck join down into the garment.

Cowl

The collar is a very wide piece of bias fabric with one edge attached to the neck of the garment. A cowl is usually attached to a low neck so an opening in the collar is unnecessary although there is sometimes a zip in the back of a dress below the cowl. Very successful in jersey fabric.

Fold the collar and join with a narrow seam. Turn a narrow hem along one edge, machine, hand sew or hold with Wundaweb (fig 4.26).

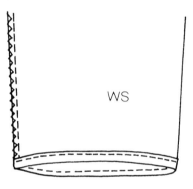

Fig 4.26

Place collar to neckline with the right side to the wrong side of the garment. Match the seam to the centre back and match the centre fronts. Pin at intervals. Tack and machine. Trim the turnings to 5 mm and zig-zag to neaten. Press the join down on to the garment (fig 4.27). Fold collar down.

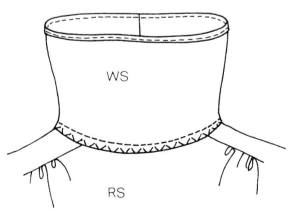

Fig 4.27

Fold-down collar

This type of collar, e.g. shirt collar, may be a rectangle of fabric folded at the outer edge, or it may be shaped, in which case the collar is cut in two pieces and joined at the outer edge.

Single layer method

With a folded collar cut iron-on Vilene the same size and press it to the wrong side of the fabric. Mark the centre back of the collar (fig 4.28).

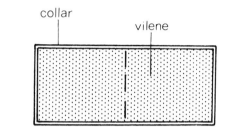

Fig 4.28

Place the right side of the collar to the wrong side of the neck, match the seam allowances and centre back marks. Pin and tack. Machine across the neck but leave the seam allowance free at the centre front. There may already be a zip in position so the stitching will cross the top of the zip and the seam allowance of the collar will extend beyond that (fig 4.29).

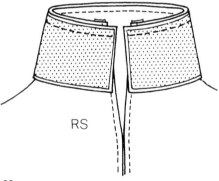

Fig 4.29

Trim the turnings, snip every 5 mm right up to the machining and press the seam open and then into the collar.

Stitch the collar ends. Either fold the collar right-sides together, stitch across the ends, trim and turn through, or, fold the collar wrong-sides together, turn in the edges to meet each other, and slip stitch. The second method is more accurate and easier to do (fig 4.30).

Fig 4.30

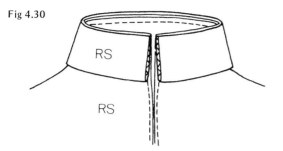

Roll the collar into the position it will take up in wear and work a row of diagonal basting along it through both layers. Trim the remaining raw edge of the collar so that only 5 mm extends beyond the row of machine. Turn under the raw edge to cover the stitching and tack. Finish by hemming or machining on the edge (fig 4.31).

Fig 4.31

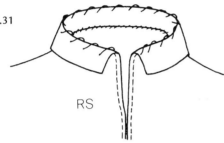

Double layer method

If the collar is in two pieces begin by trimming 2 mm from all edges of one piece. Attach iron-on interfacing to the wrong side; this is the under collar.

> TIP For a crisp shirt collar also attach iron-on Vilene to the top collar. Transparent Vilene is usually suitable.

Place top collar and under collar right-sides together, tack and machine round the outer edge. Make the raw edges meet and stitch with the top collar uppermost, taking the original seam allowance. The under collar is smaller in order that the collar rolls correctly. Trim the seam allowances, snip the outer edge turnings, cut off the corners and turn the collar right-side out. Roll the edges well and press. Edge stitch the collar if you wish. Bring the raw edges together at the neck and tack together (figs 4.32 and 4.33).

Attach to the neckline in the same way as the bias

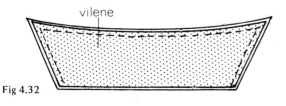

vilene

Fig 4.32

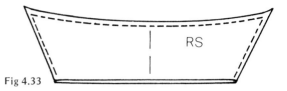

Fig 4.33

roll, folding the facings back on to the right side of the garment first.

Alternatively, when joining the collar pieces, stitch only to the seam allowance at the centre front corners. Turn and press the collar and attach by the single layer method described for the one-piece collar. Edge stitching can be added after the collar has been attached (fig 4.34).

Fig 4.34

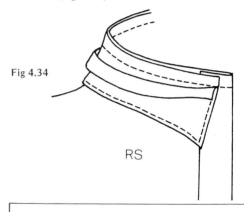

RS

> TIPS It is easier to attach the collar soon after working the shoulder seams because you can arrange the neckline flat on the table to pin the collar.
>
> Save time by pinning the collar to the garment neckline to see that it is the right length. If too long unpin and trim a little off each end of the collar. Proceed to interface and attach.
>
> If the collar meets edge to edge at the centre back, hold the two edges together with a small piece of Velcro. Hem one piece extending from the collar, the other piece under the edge it meets (fig 4.35).

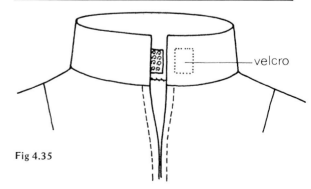

velcro

Fig 4.35

5 Machine stitching

As stitches are the means of holding the fabric together, if you take any short cuts by using big stitches or by not fastening off thread ends securely, it will in the end be time wasted, not saved. However, with hand sewing it helps to know which are the most useful stitches to learn and perfect, and where machining is concerned there are plenty of tips to help make sure that what you do is right the first time and will not need unpicking.

Obviously the greatest saving of time comes with making maximum use of the sewing machine. A certain amount can be done with a straight stitch but to have the choice of operations offered by a swing needle machine speeds up the sewing a great deal. With a fully automatic machine your whole approach to garment construction should alter. Sometimes people say that they feel they won't need embroidery stitches anyway, but a number of those stitches can be brought into beneficial use. If you vary the width and length, use them for different purposes, put different stitches together, and regard them as variations rather than embroidery, you will see how versatile they are.

The machine can be used for two kinds of stitching apart from decorative embroidery and repairs: temporary and permanent.

TEMPORARY STITCHING

There are three main temporary stitches, all inserted to hold fabric in position until a permanent stitch replaces them.

Tailor tacking

Use for marking seam allowances, etc. Work the stitching beside the edge of the paper pattern after cutting out, but before removing the pattern. Make sure there are no pins near the edges of the pattern. If the pattern has seam allowances, the edge of the paper should be folded back to 2 mm beyond the fitting line.

As this method of marking inserts a lot of tufts of thread and they have to be removed later, confine its use to areas where long seams require marking rather than points or corners. Insert a No. 80 needle and then attach the tailor tacking foot to the machine; thread with Atlas tacking thread. Set the zig-zag width to No 2. Set the stitch length on 4. Before stitching loosen the top tension, remembering to return it to the correct position after stitching. Take the top thread through the foot and then fit it into the slot and pull it out to the left to start. Stitch. The thread is lifted over the central bar of the foot, forming big loops. After stitching part the layers of fabric and nip the threads (fig 5.1).

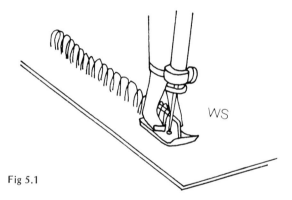

WS

Fig 5.1

Basting

This is also called machine basting or tacking.

Insert the needle with two eyes, the Magic Needle, and the zig-zag foot. Thread the machine with Atlas tacking thread and thread the upper eye.

Set the zig-zag width to maximum (4) and the length to 2½ or 3. Move the needle to the far left position and set the automatic pattern lever to blind stitch (fig 5.2).

Place pieces of fabric with right sides together and pin across the seam. Place the fabric under the foot, and if the stitching is to withstand the strain of fitting reverse at the start but with the width of stitch set on 0, then set to No. 4 to baste. Hold the fabric fairly taut in front and behind the foot, removing the pins as you approach them. The stitching forms on the left of the foot where the needle is positioned.

Fig 5.2

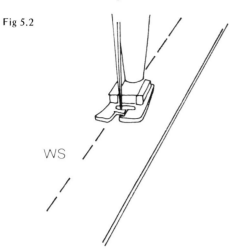

Work permanent stitching beside the basting nearer the raw edges.

When ready to remove the basting, snip the reversing at both ends, take hold of the spool thread and ease gently out.

Large straight stitch

A quick way of inserting a gathering thread, a method of marking a line and also a useful stitch for holding fabric together for fitting if your machine doesn't adapt to basting.

Thread the machine in the usual way with normal sewing thread. Adjust to the biggest stitch the machine will make. Leave reasonably long ends of thread when starting and finishing so that there is plenty to grasp when the time comes for removing the stitches. If you are doing a lot of big stitching it is worth spending a moment threading the machine with thread of a contrasting colour to make it easy to distinguish

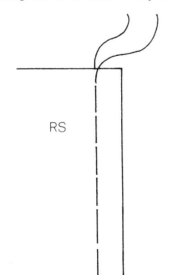

Fig 5.3

it after permanent stitching has been put in. Do not stitch too close to the raw edges of woven fabric or they will fray when you remove the thread (fig 5.3).

When marking or inserting a thread for pulling up, work with the right side of the fabric uppermost. When you remove the thread, pick up the spool thread, the one on the wrong side, and it will pull out easily.

When used as a temporary holding stitch work the permanent stitch just beside it so that removal of the large stitch is easy (fig 5.4).

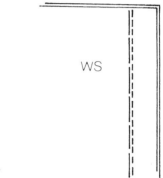

Fig 5.4

PERMANENT STITCHING

Unlike temporary machining, permanent stitches must be exactly the right size for fabric, the correct type of stitch must be selected and it must be accurately placed and the thread ends securely finished off.

Select the stitch and try it out on a double piece of fabric. Adjust the machine setting until the stitch looks satisfactory on the fabric on both sides. Unless there is something wrong with the machine the stitch will always hold the layers of fabric together satisfactorily.

The tension should not need adjusting except sometimes on exceptionally heavy or fine fabrics, although the best machines have an in-built tension adjustment that works automatically.

It is vital to use the correct type and size of machine needle. Fine needles are now used much more than previously. Fabrics are constructed and finished in a variety of ways and keeping a selection of all the needles available ensures good results. It is often only by trying the stitch that it is possible to determine which needle is best. The needle should slide easily into the fabric without breaking its construction and without noise. The ordinary sharp pointed needle is satisfactory for use on woven fabrics but some jersey fabrics made from synthetic fibres are so closely knitted that the needle cannot penetrate properly. This means that the top and bottom threads cannot lock together and so a stitch is not formed. The solution is to use a ball-pointed needle. As its name implies it is round instead of sharp and it eases its way between the loops of knitting. The principle is similar to that of the rounded point of a knitting needle that slides easily in use; if a sharp pointed needle were used it would not slip so easily between stitches (fig 5.5).

Fig 5.5

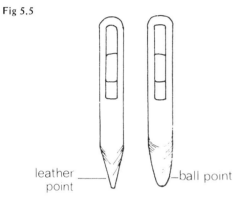

leather point _____ ball point

Leather, suede and plastic should be sewn with a spear-pointed machine needle. It has a very sharp three-sided cutting point that makes a small slit in the fabric. An ordinary needle might stitch satisfactorily but the point would force round holes in the material which would be weak and liable to tear with thread movement whereas the cut edges made by the spear close up round the thread and grip it, preventing movement.

The chart on page 48 is a guide to the size and type of needle required for various fabrics, but remember to try out a row of machining first on spare fabric before working on the garment. It saves time in the long run. If the stitching disturbs the weave or makes holes, use a finer needle. If the machine makes a noise or the needle makes a popping or bumping sound use a finer needle. If the machine fails to form a stitch change to a ball-point needle. If the fabric wrinkles place a piece of tissue or fine typing paper under the fabric before stitching. If there seems something radically wrong with the stitching, unthread the machine and start again, checking the threading procedure in your instruction book. If the threads tangle or knot at the start of stitching, remove the spool plate and spool and clean out fluff beneath with a small brush.

Starting and finishing

Always have the needle at its highest point when inserting and removing fabric.

Make sure the fabric is right under the foot at the start.

Lower the foot and turn the wheel to lower the needle into the fabric before starting to stitch. To anchor the threads reverse for two stitches before going forwards.

At the end of a row of stitching stop just before the raw edge or it may wrinkle, reverse for two stitches and remove the fabric after raising the needle.

Always remove the fabric towards the back so that the thread runs against the foot otherwise the needle may bend or break.

The cutter blade is situated at the back of the foot so use it to quickly cut the threads. Cut off close to the fabric but leave ends of 10 cm on the machine. With the work and your hands still in this position behind the foot quickly turn the fabric round and cut the thread ends that were left at the start of the seam. This is quicker than searching for them later.

> **TIP** If you cannot reverse on your machine or you do not wish to have the double stitching, drop a spot of Fray-Check liquid on to the thread ends.

Straight stitch

The stitch should appear similar on both sides of the fabric. Never use a very small stitch even on fine fabrics as it tends to compress the fabric. The best stitch is the one that appears to lie on the surface and yet can be seen locked between the two layers when the fabric is parted. A stitch that is too long will cause wrinkling and will not hold the layers together.

Zig-zag stitch

A very slight zig-zag stitch should be used for seams on jersey fabrics and others with give, including lacy or open weaves. The dial should be moved so that it is only just off 0 and the resulting stitch should look like a straight stitch. If it doesn't then you have gone too far on the dial.

A wider zig-zag is used for working over raw edges but keep the width to the minimum or it appears ugly. A very wide stitch is no more effective than a narrow one. Keep the stitch short in length too, but not so close that it forms a firm ridge.

A good zig-zag stitch is one that looks neat, with the proportion of the length to width set so that the stitch is effective but flat. As it is often worked on a single layer of fabric, the right and wrong sides of the stitching may not be exactly alike in appearance.

Sizes of machine needle and stitch

Fabric	Stitch size	Needle	Fabric	Stitch size	Needle
Barathea	Medium-large	90 (14)	Lamé	Medium	70 (11)
Batiste	Small	70-90 (11-14)	Lawn	Small	70 (11)
Bedford cord	Medium-large	100 (16)	Lurex	Medium	70 (11)
Bonded fabrics	Large	90 (14)	Madras	Medium	70 (11)
Bouclé	Medium-large	90 (14)	Moire	Medium	70 (11)
Brocade	Medium	70-90 (11-14)	Mungo	Medium	90 (14)
Calico	Medium	90 (14)	Muslin	Small	70 (11)
Camel cloth	Large	100 (16)	Needlecord	Medium	70 (11)
Challis	Medium	70 (11)	Ninon	Medium	70 (11)
Chambray	Medium	79-90 (11-14)	Ombre	Medium-large	70 (11)
Cheesecloth	Medium	70 (11)			Ball-point if
Chenille	Large	100 (16)			necessary
Chiffon	Small	70 (11)	Organdie	Small	70 (11)
Cire	Small-medium	70 (11)	Panne	Medium	70 (11)
Corduroy	Medium-large	90 (14)	Percale	Medium	70 (11)
Crêpe	Medium	70-90 (11-14)	Plisse	Medium	(70 (11)
Damask	Medium	90 (14)	Polyester/Cotton	Medium-large	70-90 (11-14)
Denim	Medium-large	90 (14)	Poplin	Medium	70 (11)
Doeskin	Medium-large	90 (14)	PVC	Large	90 (14)
Donegal	Medium-large	90-100 (14-16)	Reversible cloth	Large	100-110 (16-18)
Drill	Large	110 (18)	Sailcloth	Medium-large	90 (14)
Duck	Large	100 (16)	Sateen	Medium	90 (14)
Dupion	Medium	70 (11)	Satin	Small-medium	70-90 (11-14)
Duvetyn	Medium	90 (14)	Seersucker	Medium	70 (11)
Faced cloth	Medium-large	90 (14)	Shantung	Medium	70-90 (11-14)
Faille	Medium	70 (11)	Stretch towelling	Medium, slight zig-zag	90 (14)
Felt	Large	90 (14)			
Fur fabric	Large	100-110 (16-18)	Suede cloth	Medium, slight zig-zag	90 (14)
Gabardine	Large	100-110 (16-18)			
Georgette	Small	70 (11)	Surah	Medium	70 (11)
Gingham	Medium	70 (11)	Taffeta	Medium-large	70 (11)
Grosgrain	Medium	70 (11)	Ticking	Large	100 (16)
Habutai	Medium	70 (11)	Towelling	Large	90 (14)
Harris Tweed	Large	100 (16)	Tweed	Large	100 (16)
Jersey	Medium, slight zig-zag	70 (11)	Velvet	Medium-large	70 (11)
			Velveteen	Medium-large	90 (14)
Knit	Large, slight zig-zag	90 (14)	Voile	Small-medium	70 (11)
			Winceyette	Medium	90 (14)
Lace	Medium	70-90 (11-14)			

Fig 5.6

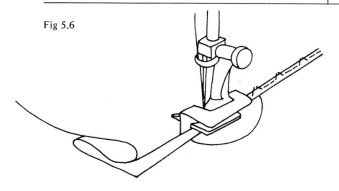

Combination stitches

Some stitches combine the straight and zig-zag movement. Select from these according to the effect you want.

The blind hem stitch makes four straight stitches followed by one zig-zag to the left. When used to fix a hem, set the zig-zag quite wide so that it catches the fold of fabric each time, but if used for decoration or on seam edges keep it narrow for neatness (fig 5.6).

The universal stitch that stitches and neatens

jersey fabrics makes one straight stitch followed by a movement to one side, another straight stitch and so on. Fabric can be lapped and stitched twice. In addition to stitching two edges in the usual way it can also be used for decoration and for seam raw edges. The overlock stitch makes two straight stitches before making one zig-zag to the right. A third stretch stitch makes four small zig-zags followed by two wider ones. This is used for open seams on stretchy fabrics (figs 5.7, 5.8 and 5.9).

Another combination stitch, the running or serpentine, is a straight stitch that runs from side to side. An attractive decoration for narrow hems and also useful for seam turnings (fig 5.10).

With all the above stitches keep the stitch length short.

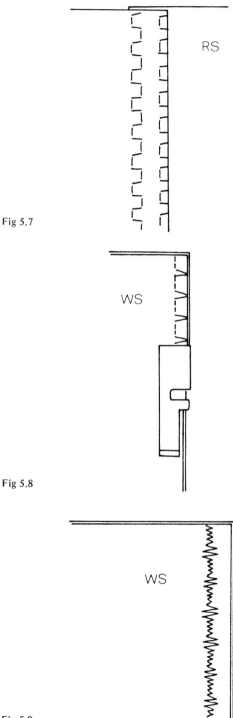

Fig 5.7

Fig 5.8

Fig 5.9

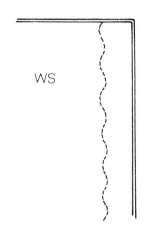

Fig 5.10

> TIP If a stretch seam flutes, feed an extra thread in under the foot. The thread is removed after the seam has been pressed (fig 5.11).

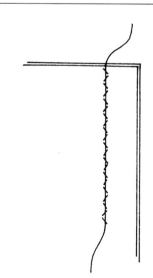

Fig 5.11

Satin stitch

Use the embroidery foot which has a wide, deep groove under the base, or, for buttonholes, use the buttonhole foot.

For satin stitch or any of the close embroidery stitches set the stitch length indicator on the line above 0, set the stitch width as required between 1 and 4. When using normal sewing thread, the satin stitch may appear too close and the fabric may not move, in which case move the stitch length indicator further from 0. Test the stitch on fabric first, putting a piece of paper underneath when working on a single layer of fabric (fig 5.12).

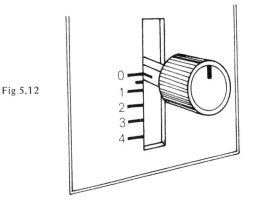

Fig 5.12

Top stitching

Effective decorative stitching can be added by using a straight, zig-zag or embroidery stitch. Adjust the length and width of the stitch according to the type of fabric.

A slightly heavier straight or zig-zag stitch can be made by using two reels of thread on the top of the macine. Use the right size needle for the fabric and place a reel of thread on each spindle on top of the machine. Thread both ends of thread

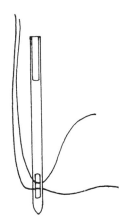

Fig 5.13

through the machine in the usual way, one at a time, and thread both through the eye of the needle. Set to a medium length stitch and sew (fig 5.13).

The double or twin needle can also be used for decorative stitching, producing shaded effects when used on very fine fabrics, a double row of stitching with a slight raised effect on opaque fabrics. Two different coloured threads can be used on the machine.

Insert the needle and thread into the machine making sure you pass the threads one each side of the tension disc but together through all the other points until you reach the needle. Insert the spool and machine in the usual way with the needle in the central position (fig 5.14).

A medium length straight stitch is very effective but so too are some of the zig-zag stitches such as the blind stitch.

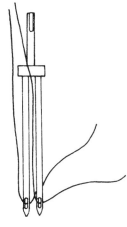

Fig 5.14

Another effective way of working decorative stitching is to work any of the zig-zag stitches or embroidery stitches to emphasise seams, edges, etc. Choose a stitch that is suitable for the type of fabric and the garment.

TIPS Contrasting colours of threads show up so it takes longer to get neat results; it is quicker to use matching thread.

Always top stitch from the right side of the garment.

Try to work through the same number of layers throughout to get the same effect.

Keep straight by using a groove or edge of the foot as a guide. Or use the grooves marked on the needle plate. If stitching further from the edge than this stick a piece of Sellotape across the machine base and use the edge as a guide (fig 5.15).

One way of working two parallel rows of top stitching is to move the needle position for the second row, but keep the foot in the same place on the fabric as for the first row (fig 5.16).

Get into the habit of removing the spool case and cover regularly to brush out fluff. It accumulates quickly because synthetic fibres and threads tend to shred and ball together. This can jam the machine if you leave it there.

Put one drop of oil in the spool socket regularly and one spot occasionally on the other moving parts you can see. If you use the machine a lot do this once a week.

Use a new needle every couple of garments; some fabrics, particularly synthetic knits, blunt the needle very quickly and it will damage the fabric, even fail to form a stitch.

If you put a special type of needle in the machine and you have to leave off for a while, write the size and type of needle on a piece of paper and leave it under the foot to remind you.

Also, when you have given the machine a thorough oiling, leave yourself a message under the foot to remind you to clean off surplus oil when you come back, before putting fabric under the machine.

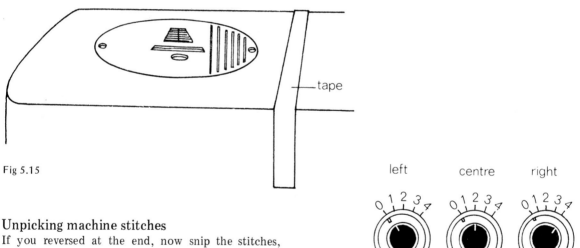

Fig 5.15

left   centre   right

Unpicking machine stitches

If you reversed at the end, now snip the stitches, pulling open the two layers of fabric apart. On reaching the single line of stitching, lift one thread with a pin, undoing about four or five stitches until you can take hold of the thread.

Hole the end of thread very firmly and tug with a sharp movement, pulling back along the stitching. The thread will break some one or two centimetres further along the line. Turn the fabric over and pick up the other thread. It will still be slightly stuck to the fabric but it is loose. Hold the end firmly and tug it back along the stitching to break the thread. Continue in this way.

Press the fabric to close up the machine holes.

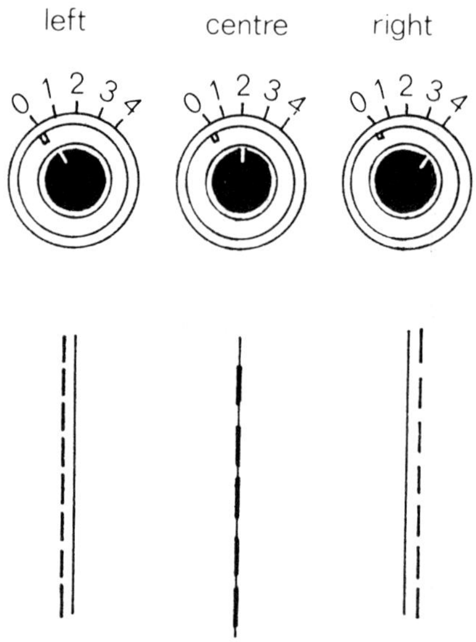

Fig 5.16

6 Some more machining ideas

Use your machine as much as you can for both functional and decorative processes. Explore the benefits that imaginative use of the basic stitches will bring. Accustom yourself to changing from straight to zig-zag, become familiar with the type of stitch that results from different setting, stitch lengths and widths so that you eliminate errors and reduce experimenting to the minimum.

Although I have made suggestions about thread and about stitch size in the machine finishes that follow, remember that both needle and stitch size must be suitable for the particular fabric that you are using. Where I have referred to 'normal sewing thread' this means the thread you are using to construct the garment, e.g. Drima.

FINE EDGING

This is suitable for all light-weight fabrics, both knitted and woven.

Prepare machine
Ordinary foot
Anchor Machine Embroidery thread No. 30 or normal sewing thread
Stitch length: ½ — ¾
Zig-zag: 1½
Trim the garment edge to 1 cm longer than needed. Turn under the 1 cm and press or tack (fig 6.1).

Fig 6.1

Place under the machine right-side up and work the machining over the folded edge. Fasten off. Cut off thread ends and carefully trim away the surplus fabric on the wrong side.

This finish is particularly useful on the edges of frills, lingerie and blouse hems (no risk of hem showing through skirt).

LACE EDGE

This is a lace extension for lingerie etc.

To attach lace edging to jersey fabric:
Prepare machine
Ordinary foot
Anchor Machine Embroidery or normal sewing thread
Stitch length: ½ — ¾
Zig-zag: 1½ — 2
Mark the position on the garment for placing the straight edge of the lace, or trim the garment edge to length plus 1 cm. With the right-side up, position the lace and zig-zag over the edge. On the wrong side trim away the surplus fabric close to the stitching (fig 6.2).

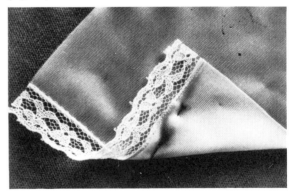

Fig 6.2

On woven fabrics set the machine for straight stitch, length 2. Mark the position for the lace or trim the edge. Place the edge of the lace in position on the right side and work the stitch evenly just within the outer edge of the lace. Fold the raw edge back on the wrong side, pulling against the stitching and press or tack and press (fig 6.3).

Fig 6.3

Set the machine to stitch length ½-¾; zig-zag 1½ and work this over the edge of the lace.

> TIP This is a good method to use when adding lace to a collar. Place the collar pieces wrong sides together, with interfacing between, attach lace to outer edge as described (fig 6.4).

Fig 6.4

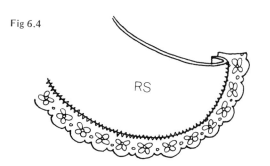

RS

SHELL HEM

Use on soft fine fabrics. Fold under the edge of the fabric and press or tack and press.

Prepare machine
Zig-zag foot
Blind hem stitch setting
Normal sewing thread
Stitch length: 1½
Zig-zag: 4

Insert fabric under the foot with the fold to the left and right side up. Work the stitch so that when the needle moves to the left it misses the fabric (fig 6.5).

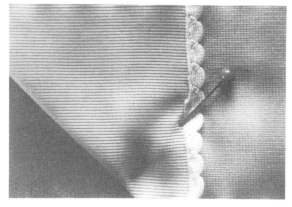

Fig 6.5

Work a second row of stitching, this time zig-zag, stitch length 1½ and zig-zag ½, about 5 mm inside the blind stitch. On the wrong side, trim away the surplus fabric close to the zig-zag.

SHELL TUCKS

Fold the fabric right-side out and press where the tuck is to be.

Prepare machine
Zig-zag foot
Blind hem stitch setting
Anchor Machine Embroidery thread
Stitch length: 1½
Zig-zag: 4

Place fabric under the foot with the fold to the left. Work the blind hem stitch so that the needle misses the fabric fold when it moves to the left.

Using an adjustable marker press another crease in the fabric parallel with the first, work a second tuck, and so on until you have sufficient. Press tucks flat.

> TIPS Work the tucks on a piece of fabric before cutting out the garment piece.
>   Make the tucks exactly on the straight grain.

SCALLOPS

Prepare machine
Satin stitch foot
Automatic pattern: scallop
Anchor Machine Embroidery thread
Paper under the fabric
Stitch length: satin stitch
Zig-zag: 3 — 4

Trim the fabric edge to 1 cm longer than needed. Place fabric on paper and under the foot. Work the stitch parallel with the trimmed edge (fig 6.6).

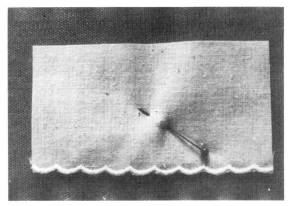

Fig 6.6

Tear away the paper. Trim away surplus fabric on the wrong side, close to the scallops.

> **TIP** A firmer edge can be produced by feeding crochet cotton No. 10 under the foot. Feed it down through the bar on the front of the machine. Make sure the needle passes at either side of the cotton as it zig-zags.

LOOP SCALLOPS

Attach to a finished garment edge, e.g. hemmed or faced. Set the machine as above and work with paper under the fabric. Position the fabric so that the needle catches the fabric edge when the far left point of the stitch pattern is reached (fig 6.7).

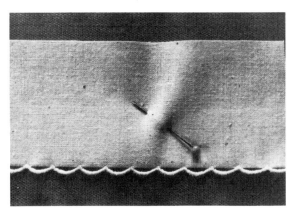

Fig 6.7

> **TIP** Make tucks with looped edges. Fold and press the fabric where the tuck is to be. Work the scallop loops on the edge. Work a row of straight stitching the width of the foot away. Press the tuck to one side. Fold and press the fabric for the next tuck and so on.

CORDED HEM

Use on any medium or heavy fabric. It can be worked at any distance from the edge but if the garment is shaped keep the hem fairly narrow.

Prepare machine

Satin stitch foot

Anchor Machine Embroidery thread or normal sewing thread

Soft Embroidery Cotton in contrasting colour

Stitch length: ½ — ¾

Zig-zag: 1½

Decide on the depth you want the hem, turn up once and press, allow 1½ cm more and trim away the surplus on the wrong side.

Attach the measuring bar to the foot and adjust it to the hem depth decided upon. Place fabric under the foot, right side up, and work the zig-zag stitch, feeding the embroidery cotton under it (fig 6.8) or work through the hole.

On the wrong side trim away the surplus fabric close to the stitching.

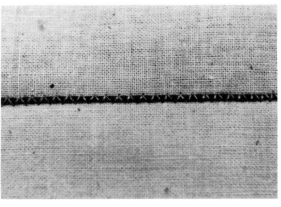

Fig 6.8

> **TIP** Unpick a section of one seam of the garment, turn up the hem and work the corded hem. Re-stitch the seam, catching in the ends of embroidery cotton. This avoids an unsightly join (fig 6.9).

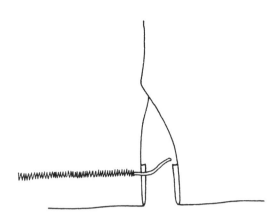

Fig 6.9

PIPED EFFECT

Use this as an alternative to piping or top stitching to emphasise an edge or a style feature.

If worked on a hem prepare it as for corded hem. If a style feature, finish the edge first, e.g. facing.

Prepare machine
Satin stitch foot
Machine Embroidery Thread
Soft cotton embroidery thread to match or tone
Stitch length: satin stitch
Zig-zag: 1½

Work in the same way as for corded hem but the satin stitch covers the embroidery cotton entirely (fig 6.10).

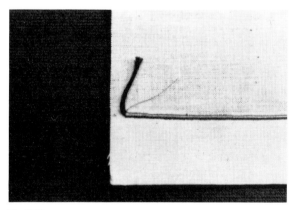

Fig 6.10

DUAL-COLOUR HEM

Use on fine fabrics. Use two different thread colours. If the fabric is printed choose two of the main colours of the print. Work parallel with any finished edge, e.g. faced or hemmed.

Prepare machine
Ordinary sewing foot
Normal sewing thread in two colours
Twin needle
Automatic pattern: blind stitch
Stitch length: ¾ — 1
Zig-zag: 2

Place the fabric under the foot right-side up and stitch parallel with the finished edge (fig 6.11).

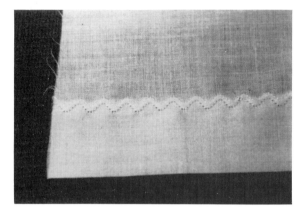

Fig 6.11

BRAID EFFECTS

Machine stitches in various colours can be added to the edges of plain ribbon or petersham ribbon. The simple stitches such as blind stitch can be used in a single or twin needle, stitching on each edge of the ribbon and also, if desired, added off the edge of the ribbon (fig 6.12).

Fig 6.12

If you use an automatic embroidery pattern choose one that does not necessarily require to be matched equally on both sides of the ribbon. Some of the larger patterns must be matched but it takes a long time to perfect the technique of doing it. It is easier to choose a smaller pattern, or a different one for each side. If, when you have worked the pattern, you feel it would be advisable to separate the two rows more, then work a third stitch, preferably an open one, down the centre (fig 6.13).

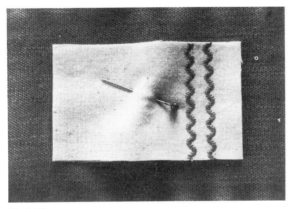

Fig 6.13

TIP If you have to make a false hem use the serpentine stitch. Butt together the raw edges of the garment and hem fabric, place a narrow strip of interfacing beneath the stitch with centre of foot over join. Work another row of stitching either side of the join. Trim away surplus interfacing. Finish the hem (fig 6.14).

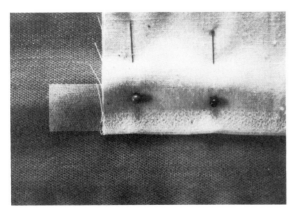

Fig 6.14

7 Seams and darts

SEAMS

Save time by using as few seams as possible. Straight pattern edges can often be pinned together before being placed on the fabric to eliminate a seam. It cannot be done with shaped seams and it should not be done if the seam is likely to be needed for fitting.

If your pattern provides a front and back yoke, place the two together at the shoulder seam and eliminate that seam (fig 7.1).

Front and back skirt pattern pieces can be cut to a fold instead of a seam (fig 7.2).

A straight or loose dress with a centre front seam

Fig 7.3

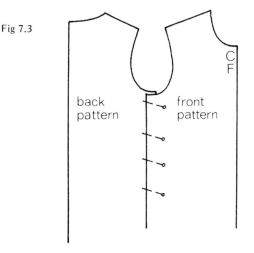

back pattern

front pattern

Fig 7.1

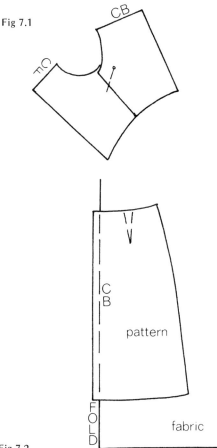

Fig 7.2

or buttoned front, can be cut without side seams (fig 7.3).

There are many more possibilities which you will discover for yourself.

Eliminating seams will alter the grain position on the garment, often making the seams that are left very much on the bias. Take care with these seams, taking note of the following points and it will not be a problem. If you are using a striped, checked or line-pattern fabric be sure that the design will be at an acceptable angle on the remaining seam before you eliminate seams.

Basic seam

Place the two pieces of fabric with the right sides together. Lift the upper layer and move it without stretching until the raw edges are together. Match up each end before settling the area between. Swivel the fabric until the seam edges are lying vertically in front of you with the wider part of the garment farthest from you.

Nearly all seams are on the bias of the fabric and it is important to stitch them in the correct direction. If you work from the widest part up to the narrow, wrinkling can be avoided and the garment seams will handle better. This last point is not so important in short seams but it is vital in long ones on dresses and skirts.

Arrange the fabric and insert pins across the seam from right to left. Use a pin about every 10-15 cms on plain fabric or one that requires no matching. Prepare as many seams as possible for machining at one time. By placing them as described there is little movement and handling so that fraying and stretching are kept to the minimum (fig 7.4).

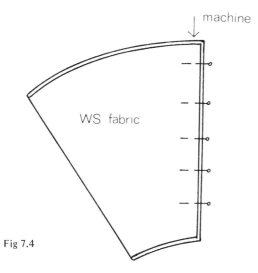

Fig 7.4

Hold the fabric flat and take it to the machine. Insert the seam under the foot, lower the foot and stitch forward for two or three stitches. Reverse for two stitches and stitch forwards. Too much reversing produces a rigid end to the seam that is difficult to press but a couple of stitches will fall within the seam allowances.

The bias edge will tend to 'give' slightly as the foot travels over the fabric. Allow the fabric to 'give' in this way. Do not stretch it as it goes into the machine but do not push it either. Use synthetic thread such as Drima in order to provide 'give' to match the seam. Remove the pins as you reach them.

When sewing on any fabric that has 'give', stitch with a very slight zig-zag stitch to ensure that there is enough stretch in the seam to compensate for the bias edge and the type of fabric. This applies to any knit fabric of any type and those of lace construction. Set the zig-zag dial to ¼.

On reaching the end of the seam stop before the raw edge appears and reverse for two stitches before removing the fabric.

> **TIP** You can save time later by cutting off all thread ends now. Use the cutter on your machine or small scissors and cut ends close to the fabric.

For check fabric or matching patterns, insert every pin very carefully, picking up a small amount of fabric exactly on the seam line. As you insert the pin make sure it is exactly on a main part of the design and check the underneath layer to ensure that the pin picks up the same part of the design. When you stitch, sew over these pins, slowly, to ensure that the fabric does not move (fig 7.5).

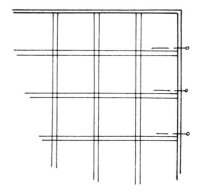

Fig 7.5

Pressing

Place the seam flat and press the stitching, then open out the fabric and arrange it on the sleeve board wrong-side up, having the hem or widest part to the right. Run the iron along the fabric with its side pressing against the line of stitching. Pull the fabric at intervals on each side of the seam to make sure that the join itself is flat against the board. Run the iron along beside it on the second side.

Using the toe of the iron, open the seam turnings. Help it by opening the turnings with the fingers of your left hand and pressing each part as you open it. Return to the right hand end and press again but using the iron flat.

By pressing in the same direction as you stitched you will avoid bubbling beside the seam.

Complete the pressing by turning the fabric over to press the right side and to remove any wrinkles you may find. Return to the wrong side and press again.

> **TIP** When pressing any pile fabric or one with a raised surface place a piece of spare fabric on the sleeve board, right-side up, and press the fabric on it with its right-side down to cushion the pile. When pressing the right side, place the spare fabric on top, pile down, before putting the damp muslin on top of that. This applies to towelling, velour, plush velvet and crêpe.

Finishing

The raw edges of the seam need neatening. This is not only to prevent fraying but also to prevent the turnings from curling up and causing a ridge.

If the fabric frays place the edge under the machine foot right-side up, turn under the edge a little and stitch with a straight stitch on the edge or a small zig-zag over the edge.

If the fabric frays but is not light enough in weight to turn under, work a medium-width short zig-zag stitch over the edge. This stitch should be small and close otherwise the fibres will still fray out between stitches. In addition, a large stitch will make the edge curl over (fig 7.6).

Fig 7.6

On jersey or knit fabrics work the blind hem stitch or the serpentine stitch along the edge to stabilise it (fig 7.7).

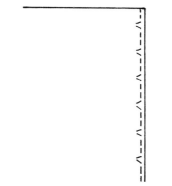

Fig 7.7

If your machine does only a straight stitch then work that on the turning 3 mm within the raw edge. It will not prevent fraying but it will stop it from going too far.

Press all seams lightly after finishing.

TIPS Whatever method of finishing you choose always stitch in the same direction, that is, from wide to narrow part of the garment.

Seams in synthetic jersey often wrinkle, especially near the hem of a skirt. Press the seam then pin the wrinkled section wrong-side up to the sleeve board. Put a pin at each end, stretching the seam. Cut a length of Wundaweb lengthwise into three and slip these pieces under the seam allowances. Press well with a hot iron and a damp muslin cloth. Allow to cool, unpin (fig 7.8).

Jersey seams running across the body must be stabilised to prevent them stretching. Cut pieces of ribbon or seam binding to the length of the seam copied from the pattern, include in the seam stitching or zig-zag to the turnings afterwards (fig 7.9).

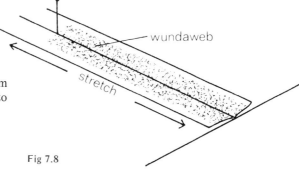

Fig 7.8

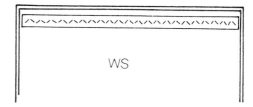

Fig 7.9

Quick seam

Machine the seam as described for the basic seam. Press the stitching flat. Trim both turnings down to 3 mm and work a small zig-zag over the edges. Work in the correct direction, removing pins as you reach them.

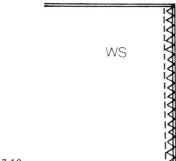

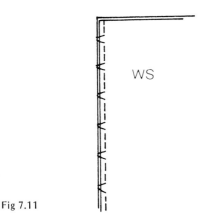

Fig 7.10

Press the seam flat then press it to one side. Press the right side of the garment to finish (fig 7.10).

One-step seam

Set your machine to the blind hem stitch and try it out on fabric to find the most suitable size. Use a small stitch, but a wide zig-zag, and Drima thread to provide 'give' (fig 7.11).

Fig 7.11

Arrange the pieces of fabric in front of you with the raw edges to the left and insert pins across the seam from the right. Trim 12-13 mm (more than 1 cm) off the raw edges. Place the seam under the machine foot and stitch with the needle passing over the raw edges when it zig-zags. Remove the pins as you reach them.

Press the stitching then press the seam to one side.

The overlock stitch on the machine also sews the seam in one movement. Use Drima thread to provide 'give'. Try the stitch on your fabric to find a suitable size. Set it to a wide zig-zag (fig 7.12).

Arrange the pieces of fabric and pin as for the basic seam. Trim both turnings down to 3 mm, cutting off a little more than 1 cm. Place under the machine and work the seam so that the needle

clears the raw edges when it moves to the right. Press the stitching, press the seam to one side.

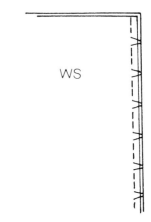

Fig 7.12

TIP If two of these narrow seams have to meet when you work a later seam, reduce the bulk and make it easier to sew by pressing the two matching seams in opposite directions. Then make sure they remain matching by inserting one pin to hold the machine over it (fig 7.13)

Fig 7.13

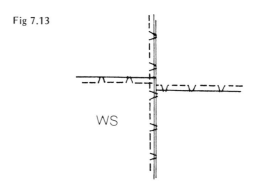

Top-stitched seams

These take longer to work because the stitching is visible.

Overlaid seam

Finish both raw edges of the fabric with zig-zag stitch or an alternative.

Decide which piece is to overlay the other — this will be the one with the stitching on. Fold this edge over on the fitting line, i.e. usually 1.5 cm, and press well.

Lay this pressed edge over the other piece of fabric, both with right sides up. Arrange the seam vertically in front of you with the overlaid piece on the left. Insert pins at intervals across the seam. Take

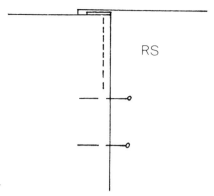

Fig 7.14

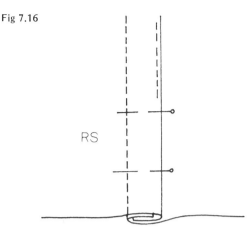

Fig 7.16

it to the machine and stitch with a medium-sized straight stitch, on the fold, very close to the edge. Remove the pins as you reach them (fig 7.14).

If you wish, work another row of stitching beside this, using the foot as a guide for keeping straight. Press the stitching on the right side and wrong side (fig 7.15).

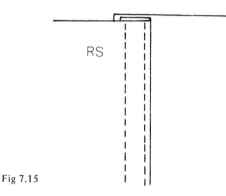

Fig 7.15

Angled seam

If your pattern shows an angled seam, the quickest way to complete it is to work it as for an overlaid seam.

Welt seam

Place the two pieces of fabric with the right sides together, pin and machine as for the basic seam. Press the turnings open to produce a good line then press both firmly to one side. Lift the top turning and trim the one underneath down to 3 mm. With the fabric flat on the sleeve board turn under and press the upper turning. To keep it level and an even width all the way along the seam tuck the raw edge under the narrow turning as far as it will go. Insert a few pins across to hold it. Machine on the fold from end to end removing the pins as you come to them. This row of stitching may be a straight stitch (make it the same size as the previous stitching) a zig-zag or a decorative machine stitch. Press both sides of the seam (fig 7.16).

Braid seam

Stitch and press open a basic seam but place the fabric with wrong sides together so that the seam turnings are pressed open on the right side. Trim down both edges to 3 mm. Place braid or bias binding centrally over the join of the seam and insert pins horizontally at intervals. Work a small zig-zag or decorative stitch over both edges, removing the pins as you stitch the first side. Work both rows of stitching in the same direction (fig 7.17).

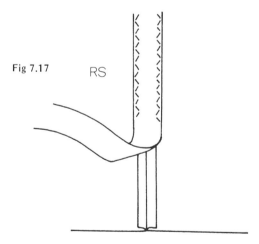

Fig 7.17   RS

Gathered seam

This seam involves gathering one edge until it is the same length as another it has to join.

Mark the points between which you are to gather by putting chalk marks on the edge of the fabric on the right side. Using the largest straight machine stitch work one row of stitching between these points, with the fabric right-side up and the stitching 1-2 mm within the seam allowance. Reverse to start

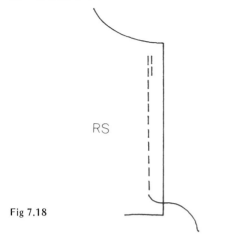

Fig 7.18

in order to anchor the ends of thread. It is only necessary to work one row (fig 7.18).

If the seam is short or you are joining two gathered edges cut a piece of tape or paper the exact length of the edge to be joined — use the pattern as a guide — and pin the ends to the edge with the gathering thread in. Pull up the gathers, holding the under thread, i.e. the one on the wrong side of the fabric, until the edge is the same length as the paper. Insert a pin in the fabric and wind the thread end round the pin. Even out the gathers. Remove the paper and pin the gathered edge to the flat edge with right sides together. Put the first pin in the centre, then add one at each end. Tack on the gathering. Remove the pins — check the other side to make sure you haven't missed any — machine with gathers uppermost 1 mm below the gathering thread (fig 7.19).

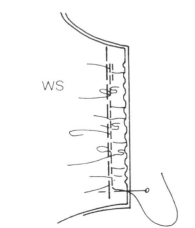

Fig 7.19

Snip the gathering thread at the anchored end and pull it out in one movement.

Press the seam so that both pieces of fabric are right side up. Do not flatten the gathers but be sure

to ease the toe of the iron along the seam to flatten the upper fabric.

Work a row of stitching on the right side parallel with the join and not too far from it — a distance of about 3 mm is usually best or the gathered edge shows as a bulky ridge. Set the machine to a straight stitch, small zig-zag or satin stitch. The corded or piped decoration described in the chapter on machine stitching is particularly suitable on medium-weight fabrics. Trim away the surplus fabric on the wrong side (fig 7.20).

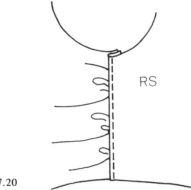

Fig 7.20

The gathered seam may also be made in the same way as an angled seam, that is, by laying one edge over the other and machining on the right side. Work a second row of matching stitching to complete it.

TIP Light-weight fabric can be gathered directly on to another piece of fabric by using the gathering foot. Use for attaching frills, etc., as the gathering cannot be precisely controlled (fig 7.21).

Fig 7.21

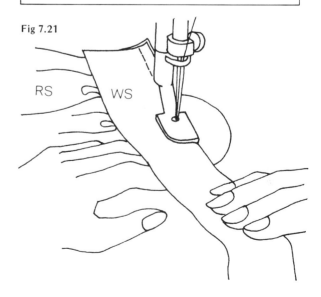

Extra-strong seam

This takes a little longer to do as there are four rows of stitching involved but it is worth it on fabrics such as cord and firm cottons.

Place the two pieces of fabric right-sides together and pin at intervals with the raw edges and the pin heads to the right. Machine, taking the appropriate seam allowance. Remove the pins.

Place the seam wrong-side up on the pressing surface and open the turnings with the toe of the iron. Press both turnings firmly to one side. Turn the fabric right-side up and press again.

Trim both raw edges to a width of 5 mm and zig-zag over both to neaten (fig 7.22).

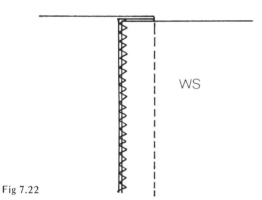

Fig 7.22

With the fabric right-side up, put it under the machine and work two rows of straight stitching, the first very close to the seam join and the second about 3 mm from it, or the width of a toe of the machine foot. If you wish to make the distance between the two parallel rows wider, leave turnings wider than 5 mm over which to zig-zag (fig 7.23).

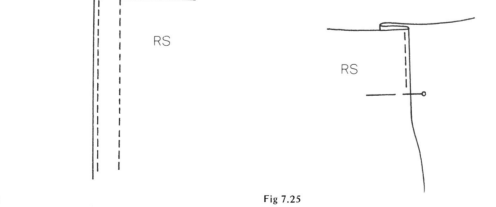

Fig 7.23

DARTS

Look at the design of the garment you are making and see whether you can make the darts into tucks. Darts are time-consuming and difficult to stitch accurately especially at the point. If you make a tuck instead you will be producing the same amount of shaping but with less trouble.

The dart should be marked on the fabric. With the fabric right-side up, fold it on one line of marking and bring it over on to the second line. Insert two pins across the tuck, having the folded edge and the head of the pin to the right. Do not attempt to make the point of the dart meet. With a long dart of perhaps 10 cm shorten it by 4-5 cm. If the dart is shorter then omit only about 2-3 cm (fig 7.24).

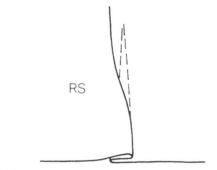

Fig 7.24

Use the toe of the iron and slide it between the pins to flatten the fold slightly. Prepare all darts to make sure pairs of tucks face in opposite directions. Pairs of tucks must be equal in length. Use tailor's chalk or wax chalk and an adjustable marker to chalk off the point at which you want to end the stitching.

Put under the machine and stitch on the edge of the fold, reversing at both ends. Remove the first pin after lowering the foot, and the second pin as you reach it (fig 7.25).

Fig 7.25

Some small darts may be omitted altogether and the surplus fabric eased into the seam. These include darts in the back neck or back shoulder, elbow darts in long sleeves and front darts in skirts and trousers.

In the case of skirts and trousers, ease in a little of the fullness but then trim away the remainder at the side seam in a gradual curve.

With neck, shoulder and elbow darts the surplus must be eased in until the edge fits the place it is joining. Pin each end and then pin at intervals between to distribute it without it forming tucks (fig 7.26).

Press the stitching flat. Arrange the dart on the sleeve board with the wrong side up and the point on the end of the board. Slide the iron beside the dart on both sides to press the stitching line against the board then press the dart to one side, pressing only to the end of the stitching, not beyond. Turn the fabric over and press the right side.

> **TIP** If you insert one pin just beyond the point of the dart it helps to keep the fabric flat as you machine.

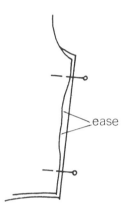

Fig 7.26

If the style and fit of the outfit would be spoiled by using tucks you will have to make darts. Fold the fabric with right sides together and, matching the two lines of dart markings, pin across the dart. Use only three pins. Use the toe of the iron to flatten the fold between the pins. Stitch. Reverse for two stitches. Remove the pins as you come to them (fig 7.27).

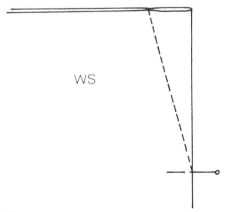

Fig 7.27

8 Buttonholes and buttons

BUTTONHOLES

You can see from the chapter on fastenings that there are a number of alternatives to buttonholes, so you will be able to avoid them on quite a number of outfits. However, if they are essential to the design or if there is no suitable and effective substitute choose one of the following types. Buttonholes in a seam are quick to do; machine-made buttonholes are quick but care should be taken; finally, piped buttonholes are time-consuming but they are the easiest of the conventional buttonholes and you cannot go wrong in their construction.

Position and size

Do not buy buttons that are appreciably larger or smaller than those recommended in the pattern, because the size of button has been considered when planning the button extension and width of facing.

The buttonhole slits should begin at a point equal to the diameter of the buttons from the edge of the garment, if they are to be horizontal. This is because when the button is fastened it settles in the end of the buttonhole, taking the strain, and it would extend over the edge of the garment if the buttonhole were too near the edge (fig 8.1).

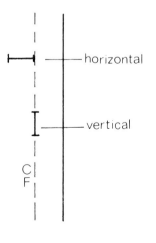

horizontal

vertical

C F

Fig 8.1

If the buttonholes are vertical they are placed on the centre front line and the buttons are attached so that they settle in the top of the buttonhole.

To prevent stretching the buttonholes in use, make the buttonholes slightly bigger than the diameter of the button. Add 3 mm for machine-made and seam buttonholes as there is very little 'give' in buttonholes and any strain would spoil them. Piped buttonholes will 'give' slightly, so allow 2 mm ease.

When using dome buttons or especially thick ones, add extra length to the buttonholes to compensate for the thickness.

Large buttons should be more widely spaced than small ones.

Decide on the position of the top and bottom buttons then space others between.

If a garment fastens up to the neck the top button should be sufficiently below the neck edge so that you do not have to work the buttonhole through the bulk of the neck turnings.

On a blouse that tucks in at the waist, avoid placing a button exactly at the waist.

If the garment is close-fitting, place a button approximately level with the bust points.

On any garment to be worn outside a skirt or trousers the bottom button should be low enough to keep the edges together in wear, but not right at the hem.

Buttonholes in a seam

The decision to make this type of buttonhole has to be made before the garment is cut out. I will describe them at a conventional centre front opening that you would find on a coat, jacket, blouse, shirt or dress; but you can apply the method to a buttonhole or a series of buttonholes in any position where you can reasonably make a seam, such as the top of a pocket. It would not be worth doing this at such points as cuffs and waistbands that are not decorative as there are other fastenings that can be employed. These buttonholes are not suitable for very light-weight fabrics (fig 8.2).

Fig 8.2

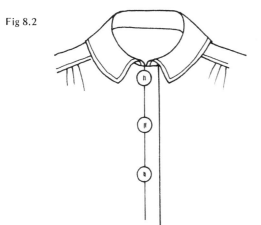

Cut the paper pattern on the centre front line. If this is not marked draw it with a pencil and ruler. Place the pattern on single fabric to cut the right side of the garment (or left for a man). Add 3 cm seam allowance at the centre front and cut out. Also cut out the other piece of pattern, adding 3 cm seam allowance. Note that this strip could well be added to the front facing before cutting, to avoid another seam on the edge of the garment (fig 8.3).

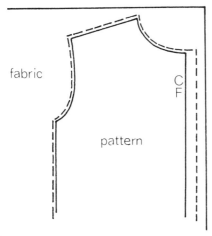

Fig 8.3

The left side of the garment should be cut from single fabric using the original pattern — you may prefer to copy it rather than cut it.

Place the extension or facing to the garment pieces right-sides together and edges meeting. Pin at intervals along the edge. Place the buttons in position, evenly spaced down the centre of the Fold-a-Band. Remember to allow a reasonable space between the neck edge and the first button. Set an adjustable marker to equal the distance between the buttons. Set another marker to the width of the button plus

ease, or establish how many perforations in the Fold-a-Band are equal to this distance, and mark with pencil the buttonhole space.

Machine down the centre of the interfacing, stopping and reversing at each buttonhole and starting again at the other side and so on. Remove pins, cut off all thread ends, press the seam open. From the right side top stitch on each side of the seam, (fig 8.4).

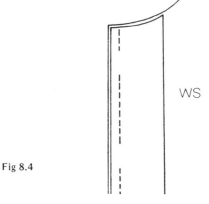

Fig 8.4

Trim down the fabric edge in the facing if it extends beyond the fold line at the edge of the garment (fig 8.5).

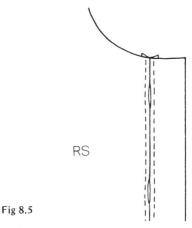

Fig 8.5

Continue with the construction of the garment until the neck is complete and the front facing has been basted in position on the wrong side.

From the right side insert a pin at each end of each buttonhole, through to the facing. Turn the garment over and, using tailor's chalk, mark these pin points with horizontal chalk marks. Remove the pins.

Cut the facing between the pins but stop the cuts 3 mm short of the chalk marks and from there cut outwards until you reach the chalk. Turn in all four

Fig 8.6

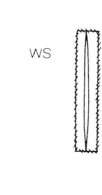

WS

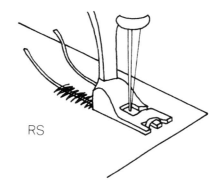

RS

Fig 8.7

sides, two long and two short, and hem into the fabric underneath with small close stitches. Press to finish (fig 8.6).

> **TIP** On fraying fabrics press a strip of Bonda-web on the wrong side of the facing to correspond with the buttonhole position. When the facing is cut fraying will be minimal.

Machine-made buttonholes

This type of buttonhole is worked through all layers, so complete the garment or at least complete all areas requiring buttonholes and work them all at one session.

In addition to interfacing, insert a strip of Wunda-web between the garment and the facing. Press well. This not only reinforces the buttonholes, but more important, it helps to prevent fraying when the buttonholes are cut.

Mark the buttonhole positions with tailor's chalk and a ruler. If they are to be vertical, draw a vertical line and mark off the buttonhole sizes with horizontal dashes. Use two adjustable markers for accuracy, one set to the buttonhole size and one to the size of the space. Alternatively cut pieces of card to measure with.

Horizontal buttonholes are more difficult to mark. Begin by ruling two parallel vertical lines; the distance between them must be exactly the size of the button-hole. Mark the buttonhole positions with horizontal chalk lines across the parallel lines. The buttonholes should be on the straight grain.

Set your machine to the correct stitch for button-holes. Attach the buttonhole foot. Thread up the machine, preferably with machine embroidery thread, e.g. Anchor. Have a gimp thread ready if you are working on medium or heavy fabric. The gimp can be double-stranded embroidery thread, a crochet cotton or tailor's gimp (fig 8.7).

Work the buttonholes following the instructions in the machine hand-book; work round twice if using machine embroidery thread.

Snip off all ends of thread. Brush off the chalk and press well on both sides of the garment. Cut the buttonholes, using the points of small scissors or, if they are not sharp enough, use an unpicker but insert a pin at each end of the buttonhole to prevent the unpicker slipping too far.

> **TIP** Prepare a piece of fabric and work a test buttonhole before you start. Cut it and try it for size before making them on the garment.

Piped buttonholes

Suitable for almost any fabric, this is a method of making piped buttonholes using one piece of fabric which makes them slightly quicker to do.

The first stage should be worked as early in construction as possible because it helps to have the fabric flat on the table to attach the pipings.

Attach interfacing to the wrong side of the fabric and mark the buttonhole positions on the right side with tailor's chalk, as described for machine-made buttonholes.

Make the piping by cutting a strip of fabric on the straight grain 3 cm wide. It should be long enough to allow 3 cm of piping for each buttonhole, more if your buttons are more than 2 cm in diameter. If your fabric is very fine, cut the strip 3 cm wide.

Cut a strip of Bondaweb the same width and press it to the wrong side of the strip. Peel off the paper backing and fold the raw edges in to meet each other. Press well with the raw edges together (fig 8.8).

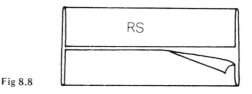

RS

Fig 8.8

Place the piping on the right side of the garment. Leave at least 5 mm extending beyond the chalk line at each end, tack in the middle of the strip. Make sure the cut edges are on the chalk line.

As you have now covered the chalk lines marking the size of buttonhole, re-chalk across the pipings.

Set your machine to a small stitch to make it easier to make all buttonholes exactly the same size. Stitch the piping to the garment by machining in the centre of each side. Stitch exactly to the chalk marks. Begin in the middle of the piece and stitch to the end, turn, stitch to the far end, turn and return to the middle. This manoeuvre provides extra firmness but it also means that you can snip off all thread ends with safety. Remove tackings (fig 8.9).

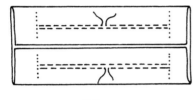

Fig 8.9   RS

Turn the work so that it is wrong-side up and snip between the rows of stitching through the garment but not through the buttonhole piece. Make a small snip and then cut out to all four ends of stitching. On the right side, cut the buttonhole piece along the centre to separate it into two pipings. Push these pipings through to the wrong side and manipulate them with your fingers to flatten the ends of the rectangle now showing. Tack together the two edges of piping. Push the triangle of fabric at each end through to the wrong side and stab stitch back and forth on the fold from the right side to hold it down. Press the buttonhole from both right and wrong sides (figs 8.10 and 8.11).

Fig 8.10

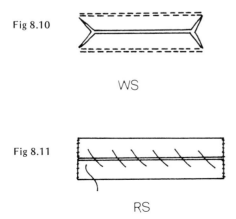

WS

Fig 8.11

RS

The buttonhole may be machined across the ends and between the piping and the garment. This is not necessary for strength but it helps to hold down springy fabrics. In addition, if there is top stitching elsewhere on the garment then this will match (fig 8.12).

Fig 8.12

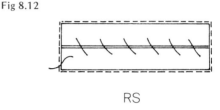

RS

Leave the buttonholes and continue with the construction of the garment. The buttonholes may be finished at any time after the facings are in position. When you are ready to complete them, proceed in the following way.

Before folding the facing back against the garment press a strip of Bondaweb to the wrong side. Cut the strip wide enough and long enough to cover all the buttonholes. Peel off the paper (fig 8.13).

Fig 8.13

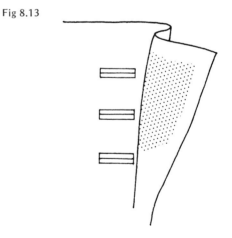

Place the facing in position against the garment and pin or tack round each buttonhole from the right side through the garment and through the facing. Insert a pin through each end of each buttonhole. The points extend through the facing, indicating the exact size of the buttonhole. Snip between the pin-points, remove the pins, turn the edge of the slit under and hem with small stitches to attach the fold of the facing to the back of the buttonhole (fig 8.14). Press well on both sides to finish.

Fig 8.14

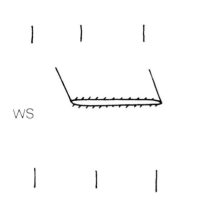

WS

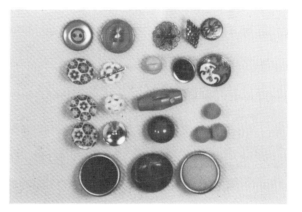

> **TIPS** Count the number of machine stitches used on the first buttonhole and make sure all are the same size.
>
> The facing on the back of the buttonhole may be cut in the same shape as the buttonhole was cut, and the edges turned in to form a rectangle.
>
> If working on check or striped fabric cut the buttonhole piece on the cross to avoid having to match the pattern.

BUTTONS

There is no short cut to sewing on a button. If it is not sewn really well it will quickly come off. However, there are a few tips that make the job much easier.

Needle

Use a larger size needle than the one used for hand-sewing on the remainder of the garment, but make sure it will pass through the fabric without difficulty.

Thread

Use synthetic thread such as Drima. It is strong but fine and will wear well. It may well be the thread you have used for making the garment.

Alternatively, on thick fabrics and outer wear use button thread, such as Anchor, or use Heavy Duty thread. They are thick, strong glazed threads specially made for the purpose.

Reinforcing

Make sure there is a layer of interfacing between the two layers of fabric. On heavy fabric or on clothes which will receive hard wear it is wise to also add a small piece of cotton fabric to stitch through. Raincoats, overcoats and suede and leather coats may have a small backing button sewn on the wrong side attached at the same time as the main button. This will prevent the fabric being torn if the button comes off.

Preparing the garment

Try to ensure that sewing on the buttons is the very last job of all because they get in the way if attached too soon and also pressing is difficult.

Press the entire garment — this is its final press — and hang it to cool.

Arrange it on the table without creasing, establish the button position then draw that part of the garment towards you and sew on the buttons. Try not to crush any part as you sew. Probably the best position is to stand up to do it to avoid the temptation to crumple the garment on your lap. Raise the work by using the sleeve board, lifting only the part of the garment needing a button, on to the board.

Preparing the thread

Cut off a piece of thread about 40 cm long, thread the needle, put in a knot to join the ends. Run your cake of beeswax along the thread several times. To do this, hold the knot and run the wax from knot to needle to avoid an uneven double thread. Without letting go of the knot, put down the wax and twist the thread by rubbing the palm of the outer hand firmly across the thread. This will twist the thread. Wind that twisted section round the thumb holding on to the knot and rub your palms together again. Continue until you reach the needle (fig 8.15).

Unwind the twisted waxed thread from your thumb.

Marking the position

Lap one side of the opening over the other, making

Fig 8.15

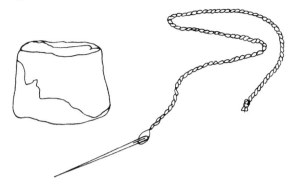

sure any centre front lines, etc., are matched up. If the button is to be attached to a waistband or some other close-fitting area, try on the garment and mark the position of the overlap with a pin.

Insert pins through the garment between the buttonholes to hold. Mark the exact position for attaching the button, using a chalk pancil inserted in the top of a vertical buttonhole, or with a horizontal buttonhole, in the end taking the strain of fastening. Begin by sewing on the bottom button if there are several. Mark only one at a time (fig 8.16).

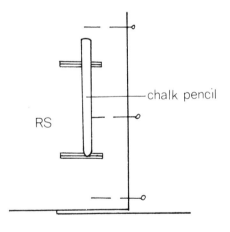

chalk pencil

RS

Fig 8.16

Sewing on buttons

Remove the pin anchoring that part of the opening, remove the top layer of garment, insert the prepared needle exactly on the chalk mark. Take two stitches right through all layers, stabbing the needle back and

forth and finally bringing it back to the right side of the garment. Cut off the knot in the thread (fig 8.17).

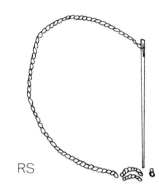

RS

Fig 8.17

Slip the button on to the needle. Insert the needle through the other hole in the button into the garment and out again all in one movement. Pull the thread through and adjust the button — it should not be flat on the fabric but because of the sewing action it stands up on its side, the advantage being that this position ensures extra thread between button and garment. With thick fabrics this extra amount of thread will have to be adjusted and made up to 5 mm long. The shank must be long enough to allow the total thickness of the other layer of garment to lie flat between the button and the garment (fig 8.18).

Fig 8.18

RS

Bring the needle up through the first hole of the button.

Insert it in the second hole, down into the garment and up again below the button. Adjust the thread and button to get the shank threads the same length.

Continue in this way until six stitches have been worked. When sewing on buttons with four holes, make four stitches across one way and then move the needle to the second pair of holes and work three stitches.

You will finish with the needle under the button. From that position take hold of the thread near the button and wind it round the shank to cover it. Wind twice more, nearer to the button and pull hard, then twice more moving back down to the garment (fig 8.19).

Fig 8.19

RS

The thread is now near the fabric again. Take two stitches across the base of the shank, through the threads and through the surface of the fabric. Pull the thread tight. Pass the needle to the wrong side or underneath and take two stitches. Cut off the thread close to the surface of the fabric. Fasten the button, mark the position of the next one, unpin and undo the button already attached. Sew on the next button, and so on (fig 8.20).

RS

Fig 8.20

When all buttons are sewn on press the area by running the toe of the iron round and underneath each button.

Buttons without through-holes

The buttons may be designed to have the needle and thread passed through a tunnel on the under-side. Attach by working six stitches, leaving a shank in the way already described.

Buttons with a shank

These are buttons, often metal or elaborate plastic ones, with a metal loop on the back. The needle should be passed through it six times for a small button, eight for a large one. Do not make a thread shank, sew the button flat to the fabric but tidy up the stitches by winding the thread round between the metal loop and the fabric before fastening off.

Decorative buttons

If the button is decorative, sew it in position using only four stitches before passing the needle across the base to finish off. Do not make a shank; do not wind the thread round the stitches and instead of fastening off on the wrong side, snip the thread after passing the needle across the base of the stitching.

TIPS When preparing the thread, make up one needle of waxed thread before you start for every two buttons to be attached. This will ensure that you use enough stitches and are not tempted to skimp the process.

Each double thread should be about 50 cm long when twisted.

Try to make the stitches fall roughly on top of each other so that they look tidy on the under side of the garment. When complete, before cutting off the thread work loop stitch over these stitches to form a neat bar. If the button has four holes work about three loop stitches across the centre of the threads.

---

9 Zips and fastenings

ZIPS

Avoid the methods of insertion that take time and extreme care to get right, mainly those where you fight to cover the zip so that it does not show. Confine yourself mainly to the concealed zip, specially made to be invisible and very easy to put in, and when using other zips with visible teeth, make a feature of the zip (fig 9.1).

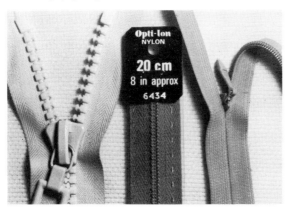

Fig 9.1

Concealed zip

The lightest and most supple zips are made of nylon coil attached to tape. The zips are made in lengths of 20 and 23 cm for skirts and trousers and 56 cm for dresses. The range of colours is not extensive, containing a few pale colours, some medium tones and the usual dark colours, but the colour match is not too important because the zip does not show in wear.

Use at the side or front of skirts and trousers and at the back or front of dresses.

Sew in by hand using backstitch or fit the one-sided zip foot (piping foot) on the machine. It does not require a special foot.

Stitch the garment seam. The gap left should be 1 cm shorter than the length of the zip teeth but you may find it easier to stop the stitching 3 cm below this. Change the machine stitch to the largest size and machine from that point to the top of the zip position (fig 9.2).

Fig 9.2

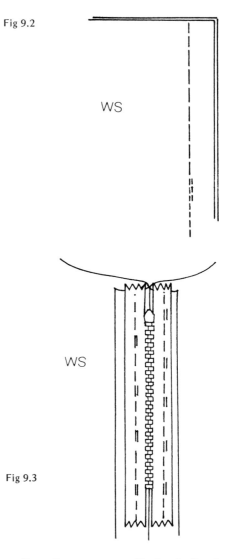

WS

WS

Fig 9.3

Press the seam open. Neaten both edges from top to bottom.

With fabric wrong-side up, place the zip right-side down on the seam. Make sure the zip slider is a fraction below the fitting line of the garment. Tack from top to bottom on each side but tack through the zip tape and the seam allowance. Prevent the needle from penetrating the garment beneath by sliding your fingers under the seam allowance. Take a back stitch every third stitch as this zip has a tendency to slide out of place. Make sure the centre of the teeth lies exactly over the seam line (fig 9.3).

Remove the large machining and stitch the zip to the turnings. To do this, roll the teeth over as flat as possible so that the stitching can be placed as close to the teeth as possible. Use a medium-length machine stitch and sew with the zip teeth uppermost. Stitch as far as possible. The slider will be in the way at the bottom so stop machining. Stitch the other side in the same way. Remove the tacking stitches (fig 9.4).

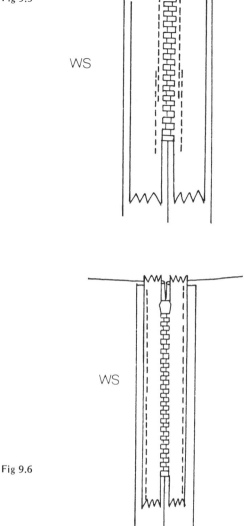

Fig 9.5

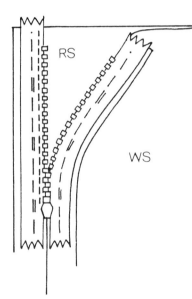

Fig 9.4

Fig 9.6

Close the zip, running the slider slowly to roll the teeth over gently. Stick a length of Sellotape over the join on the right side, taking it from below the gap in the seam to a point about 5 cm along the zip. Turn the garment wrong-side up, lift the lower end of the zip and slip stitch by hand to close the gap from below the zip stitching to the top of the seam stitching. Pick up a small amount of fabric from each fold of fabric alternately. Do not pull the thread tight. Fasten off. Re-tack the bottom part of the zip tape to the seam allowances and stitch as close as possible to the teeth. If the machine still has the zip foot on you can do this by machine. If not, back stitch by hand. Remove the Sellotape and tacking (fig 9.5).

If you stitch the entire zip by hand and you are doubtful of its strength, machine as well, stitching on the edge of the tape, attaching it to the seam allowance (fig 9.6).

Visible zips

Use a conventional zip of nylon or metal with coloured teeth. Choose a matching or contrasting zip. There is a wide range of colours in all lengths up to 56 cm.

Zip in a seam

This method is suitable only for the centre front of a garment, or in an asymmetrical front seam. The main difficulty in putting in a zip is that the fabric is so much lighter in weight and different in texture from the zip tape. You can overcome this problem by having ready two pieces of soft iron-on Vilene 2 cm wide and 3 cm longer than the zip.

Stitch the garment seam to the zip base point. Press it open and neaten both edges right to the top of the zip opening. Press a small piece of Bondaweb beside the stitching at the top of the seam stitching (fig 9.7).

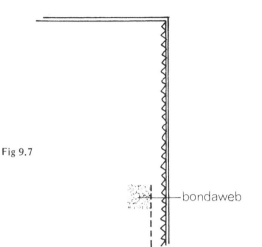

Fig 9.7

bondaweb

At the base, snip at an angle to form a triangle, the base of which is exactly equal to the width of the zip teeth. Fold the triangle to the wrong side and press (fig 9.8).

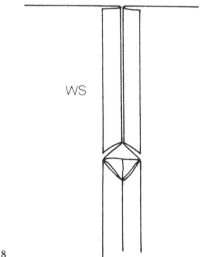

WS

Fig 9.8

Turn in the seam allowance above this and press. Open out the turnings, place the Vilene in position with one edge on the crease. Press. Fold the turnings over and press again (fig 9.9).

Fig 9.9

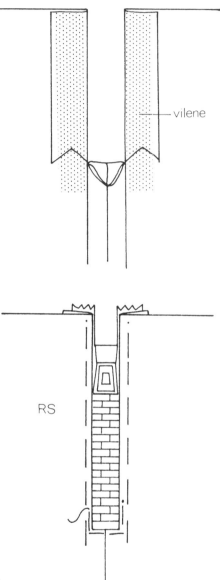

vilene

RS

Fig 9.10

Starting at the base, place the zip under the opening and tack round the end stop of the zip. The fold of the fabric should be close against the teeth. Tack along both sides of the zip in this way (fig 9.10).

Stitch, using the zip foot on the machine and a medium-sized stitch. Sew once close to the teeth and again a little distance away — about 3 mm (fig 9.11).

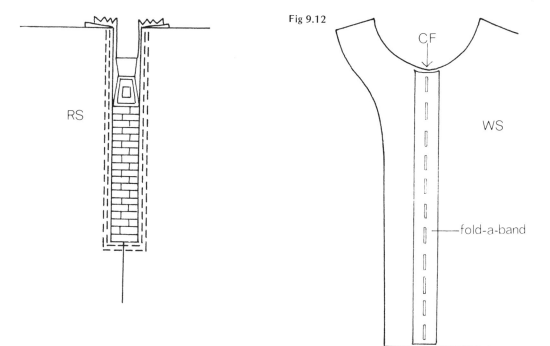

Fig 9.12

Fig 9.11

Remove tackings. Press up to the teeth but not over them.

Open-ended zip

These are available with nylon and metal teeth and there is in addition the jumbo-size Alpine zip with large plastic teeth. Colours are limited in the latter type but the others are made in a wide range of colours and lengths. Buy the zip and if necessary adjust the length of the garment to fit the zip. The zips are suitable for centre front openings on jackets, blousons, anoraks, track suit tops, etc.

It is easier if the bottom of the garment is completed before the zip is inserted.

It is usual to have a turn-back facing on the garment of about 5 cm, so add this on when cutting out if it is not allowed-for in the pattern. Neaten the facing edge and press a length of Fold-a-Band on the wrong side with the central holes exactly on the centre front line. Alternatively, press a piece of iron-on Vilene to the garment. Your decision will depend upon the edge of the garment. The facing is added for support but also to neaten the neck edge where there may be a collar. If this is so, the facing will be shaped round to the shoulder seam and therefore the Vilene should follow that shaping. The zip will not necessarily extend right up to the neck. Fold the edges back and press (fig 9.12).

Begin at the bottom and put the zip under the folded fabric edge. The bottom of the zip should be level with the bottom of the garment. Tack, holding the edge of the fabric close to the teeth (fig 9.13).

Fig 9.13

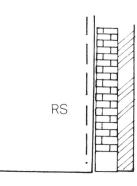

Return to the bottom and tack the other side. The ends of tape may be caught later in a neck finish but if not, trim them off to 1 cm, turn under the ends and hem.

Machine the zip with two rows of medium-sized stitching, the first close to the teeth and the second 3 mm away. Fasten off the stitching strongly, especially at the bottom of the zip where you may find it difficult to sew throught the last little bit of the tape because it is reinforced (fig 9.14).

Fig 9.14

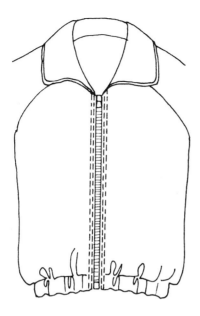

Decorative zip

Use an ordinary or an open-ended zip. This method is suitable for centre front openings. Prepare the edges as for the visible zip but turn the edges to the *right side* of the garment, tack and press and trim them down to 5 mm. Place the zip on top, on the right side of the garment. The zip tape must cover the seam allowances. Tack the zip along each side, turning under the ends of the tape. Stitch in one of the following ways.

— two rows of straight stitching, one on the edge of the tape and another 3 mm inside, in matching thread
— one row of zig-zag stitch along the centre of the tape in matching thread
— a row of machine embroidery stitching worked over the edge of the tape, in matching or contrasting thread (fig 9.15)
— one row of straight or zig-zag stitch in matching thread, covered with contrasting braid which is stitched in place along both edges by hand or machine, or, if narrow, down the centre with one row

TIPS If zip teeth seem tough, run your beeswax along them to lubricate.

Always stitch in the same direction on both sides of the zip.

If the two edges of fabric have to be exactly level, as, for example, when matching stripes

or where there is a crossing seam, stitch that part first for about 3 cm, then start again and sew the entire zip.

It is not easy to work a second row of parallel stitching using the zip foot because you have no guide. It helps to put a piece of Sellotape on the fabric with one edge marking the position of the stitching.

Even hems, ordinary zip

If you cannot use any of the methods described above, the next easiest method of insertion is by the even-hem method. Two folds of equal width meet centrally over the teeth. The teeth will inevitably show at some stage, so buy a nylon or metal zip with coloured teeth.

Try to avoid a long centre back zip — replace it with a short one in the back neck and a 30 cm zip in the left side seam.

The even-hem method is also suitable for centre front openings on dresses and trousers and side opening skirts.

If the fabric edges are straight, build up the fabric by inserting a narrow strip of soft iron-on Vilene under the turnings. It helps to allow additional seam allowances — say 2.5 cm — when cutting out (fig 9.16).

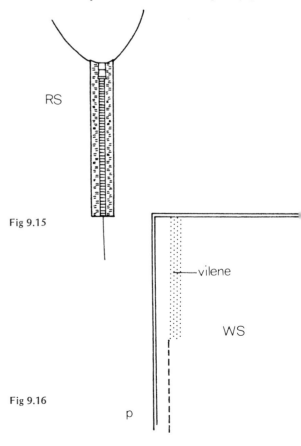

RS

Fig 9.15

vilene

WS

Fig 9.16

p

Stitch the seam to the zip base position. Press open. Neaten the seam right to the top.

Fold back the seam allowances beside the zip and press. Open out again and press the Vilene in position with one edge on the crease (fig 9.17).

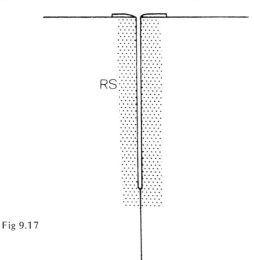

Fig 9.17

Fold turnings back and press again. With garment right-side up place the zip under one edge with the fold half-way over the teeth. Tack beside the teeth (fig 9.18).

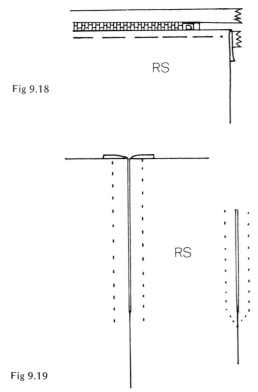

Fig 9.18

Fig 9.19

Tack the second side in the same way.

Hold the two folds together over the zip with a length of Sellotape.

Stitch in the zip with hand prick stitch or using the zip foot on the machine. Do not sew too close to the teeth. Sewing straight across below the bottom of the zip invariably produces a bulge: either work two parallel rows only, or stitch to a V to avoid this (fig 9.19).

Remove tackings and Sellotape. Press the stitching from the right side.

TIPS Always ease rather than stretch fabric on to a zip.

If you widen the seam allowance when cutting out, you can use Fold-a-Band to reinforce the edges.

When putting a zip in a side seam, stitch the seam to the zip base point, insert the zip so that the slider comes at the fitting line at the armhole. After inserting the zip, work a bar tack above the slider and finish the armholes, stitching across just above the top of the zip.

Before inserting an ordinary zip the fabric will lie flatter, especially soft fabric, if a narrow strip of Wundaweb is inserted under the pressed back edges.

FASTENINGS

In order to be effective, i.e. strong and lasting, fastenings must be sewn on well and that is time-consuming. So in order to save time, fastenings that are easy to attach must be chosen.

Velcro

Without a doubt this is the quickest of fastenings to attach, partly because you don't have to spend time locating the exact position, and partly because it is not fiddly to hold while sewing. Available in a variety of colours and three widths, it can be cut to any length or shape.

Use it to fasten waistbands of skirts, trousers and wrap-over skirts, to fasten cuffs and belts.

Use it in circles or squares in place of buttonholes. Sew the buttons on top.

Use it in short lengths in place of a zip in full skirts.

Use a tiny piece to hold collars neatly together at the back of the neck, in place of a hook.

Use it to fix anything detachable or interchangeable.

Use it to fasten straps of dungarees and pinafores, passing the end through a plastic or wooden ring.

Velcro is made of nylon so it is durable and endlessly washable. Because it is so strong, eliminate sharp corners by trimming them off if you are using squares or rectangles. Also Velcro's great virtue is its easy adjustment. As this may leave part of the hook or scratchy side exposed, always use a slightly smaller piece than the softer loop side.

It doesn't really matter which side of the Velcro is positioned where, but it prevents tights being caught when dressing if the soft side faces the body.

When using Velcro in a position where the body is liable to expansion, i.e. waistband, eliminate creaking by leaving ½-1 cm free of stitching at the open end of the band. This allows the end of the Velcro to lift instead of pull (fig 9.20).

Fig 9.20

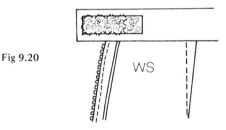

In attaching Velcro, machine large pieces if possible, provided the stitching does not show too much, or forms part of a design of stitching such as on a waistband. Set the machine to a small zig-zag stitch and work it over the edge.

If you have difficulty in keeping the Velcro still while stitching, use a small piece of double-sided tape or a spot of Copydex.

When sewing by hand use a small needle that will easily penetrate the Velcro and take small hemming stitches through the edge of it. If you find it difficult the reason is either the needle is too big or your stitches are too big (fig 9.21).

Always use Drima because it is strong.

Fig 9.21

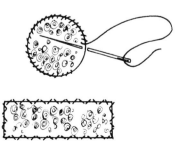

Ties

Ties can be made from fabric, bias binding, cord or flat braid. Use them in place of buttons and buttonholes, frog fastenings and on any edge-to-edge neck opening.

Narrow bias ties can be made in the same way as a tube or rouleau belt or belt loops.

Straight ties can be any width, stitched and turned through or the strip of fabric can be turned in on both sides and then folded again and machined (fig 9.22).

Fig 9.22

Attach by folding under one end and hemming to the wrong side of the garment, or if there is a seam or join available, tuck the end in and stitch on the wrong side. This method may be used where ties are inserted in a bound edge (fig 9.23).

Fig 9.23

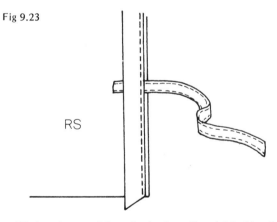

If the ties must be attached on the right side, tie a knot in the end and twirl it round a couple of times decoratively and hem in place (fig 9.24).

The raw ends of tube ties can be tucked in. This ties and cord can be knotted. The ends of flat braid should be mitred; do this by hand or machine.

Fig 9.24

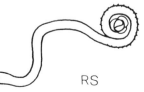

Loops

Loops to fit round buttons can be made from cord, straight or bias ties as above, or bias binding, but they should be set into a seam for neatness and they look good only with large buttons or toggles. They may be inserted in a bound edge between the binding and the garment.

If flat braid is used mitre the loop at the fold and press. Insert the loops in a seam or under a braid edge or stitch to the wrong side of the garment, turning under the raw ends of the braid and hemming (fig 9.25).

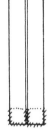

Fig 9.25

Snaps

There is a variety of metal studs available with decorative tops. Most of these are quickly attached by squeezing on to the fabric and are an excellent method of fastening.

Where several press studs are needed buy those that are fixed to tape. Attach by machining round the edge of the tape with a medium, straight machine stitch.

> **TIP** Use the zip foot so that you can stitch past the press studs easily (fig 9.26).

Trims — the press studs with metal caps that are available which need to be covered with fabric — are not really a short cut because they take a little time to prepare and attach. However, if you wish to avoid buttonholes then they are very useful.

Trouser clips

Use on waistbands of trousers and skirts.

These are big and strong and not too fiddly to attach. The best type is one with a bar with spiky prongs as it doesn't have to be stitched.

If at all possible insert the hook in the end of the waistband. Attach both hook and bar before finishing the band.

It is not easy to establish the position of the bar once the hook is in place, so mark the position with a clearly visible chalk mark, not a pin. Push the prongs of the bar through the waistband from the right side. On the back flatten the prongs.

Fig 9.26

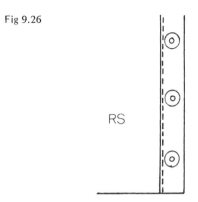

RS

If you have only a single layer of fabric through which to fix the bar, add additional strength by putting a piece of plain cotton fabric on the back. Hold in place with a piece of Wundaweb then insert the bar.

To attach the hook cut a piece of tape or seam binding about 10 cm long. Thread the tape through the loop of the hook in a swing-ticket knot. Place the hook in position at the end of the waistband on the outer part of the band but on the wrong side. Use double-waxed thread and oversew firmly round the holes on each side of the hook. Pull the tape back and lay it flat on the waistband. Hold it down firmly with plenty of hemming stitches. Tuck the waistband backing under the head of the hook and oversew the two folds together between the metal parts of the hook. Finish the waistband (fig 9.27).

Note that you will not be able to machine across the end of the waistband where the hook is.

Fig 9.27

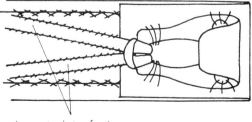

hem to interfacing

10 Edges and hems

It takes longer to make something unnoticeable than something visible, so most quick methods are ones that are visible when finished. Choose the method of finishing the edge or hem according to the weight and type of the fabric and the effect that you want.

BINDING OR CROSSWAY FINISH

Narrow strips of fabric cut on the cross or bias can be used to finish edges including necklines, armholes, front fastening edges, sleeve hems, jacket and skirt hems, edges of hoods and collars.

Purchased binding is available in a wide variety of plain colours and mainly in three widths. Pretty printed binding is available in narrow widths. The narrow binding is soft, the medium and wide ones are firmer but coarser in texture. Use narrow binding on thick fabrics; it is really too soft for fine fabrics.

Ordinary fabrics, cut into strips, are easier to use as they are firm and they are also more decorative. Keep pieces of all types of fabric including lining materials and nylon jersey; it is useful to be able to find an odd piece of matching or contrasting material, plain or print, to use for crossway strips or facings. With some uses it helps to fold over and press one edge before applying the strip. When using ready-prepared bought binding which has both edges pressed over, it often helps to remove one of these folds by pressing it out.

These strips can also be used for tie belts, rouleau ties, loops for buttons. See those sections for details.

Cutting your own binding

Strip width and direction depends on weave; follow the instructions below.

Woven fabrics

When using woven fabrics the strips are cut at an angle to the selvedge because that provides 'give' that enables you to manipulate the binding round curves. It also provides a contrast in effect to have the weave of the fabric on the bias.

The 'true' bias or true cross can be found at an angle of $45°$ to the selvedge. The easiest way to find the position is to mark a point on the selvedge and measure from that point an even distance down the selvedge and across the weft or width of the fabric. Draw a chalk line with a ruler, joining these two points, cut on the chalk line and that gives you two true cross edges (fig 10.1).

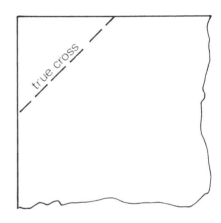

Fig 10.1

The pieces of fabric used will invariably be small scraps from which other pieces have been cut, so the edges will not be straight, but you will be able to follow a straight thread clearly enough to measure on.

Having made the first cut, decide how wide you need the strips. This will depend on the final effect, but allowing two seam allowances of 5 mm each, a strip 2-3 cm wide is about average. It can be trimmed before completion for a very narrow effect. Set an adjustable marker to the width and cut parallel with the bias cut edges of the fabric. Use cutting out shears, make long cuts holding the marker well ahead. If you use small scissors and cut slowly the strip will be uneven. If you try to chalk or pin, the fabric will bubble. If the cut strips are wildly uneven trim them after cutting (fig 10.2).

If the fabric is checked, striped or printed in a line pattern the strips will have to be cut on the true cross but if not, bias strips with a little less 'give'

Fig 10.2

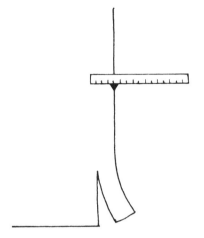

Lay out the strips wrong-side up with ends meeting. Cut one end at an angle of 45°. Cut the other to fit. Lift up both cut ends and insert a pin across the seam. Cut and pin all other joins (fig 10.3).

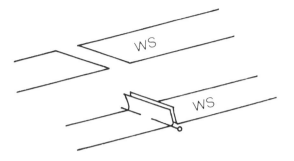

Fig 10.3

can be cut at an angle less than 45°. The advantage of having less 'give' is that pieces are easier to handle and will be less inclined to bubble when attached to straight edges. Cut in the same way, marking a chalk line for the first cut and then cutting strips from both edges.

Cut more than you need, allowing about 3 cm extra length for each join to be made.

Knitted fabrics

For special effects you may wish to cut bias strips on the cross as described for woven fabrics but the fabric is not easy to handle because there is a tremendous amount of stretch in it that can be almost uncontrollable. The exceptions to this are the firm knits such as nylon jersey, heavy polyester, knits, Raschel knits. On the whole it is the warp knit construction fabrics that will stretch most. Pull the material on the bias and see how much it stretches.

Knit fabrics also give a lot across the width, often to the same degree as on the cross and usually too much for such items as belts and rouleau loops and ties. If the fabric stretches much more than the thread then the stitches will break under the strain of being pulled.

It is usually best to cut binding strips on the warp, parallel with the selvedge on knit fabrics. This provides sufficient 'give' for most purposes. If you are unsure then cut a short piece and try it.

Joining the strips

The strips may have to be joined to make sufficient length. Even if you are using it in several different positions it is more convenient and quicker to prepare one long piece and use it as needed.

Strips of fabric whether straight or bias look best if the joins appear on the garment at an angle.

Stitch these little seams by hand or machine taking 3-5 mm turnings. Due to the way the ends have been cut, you will have an odd angle of fabric extending at both ends. This can be a useful guide for joining as the stitching must begin and end in that angle so that when opened out the strip has continuous straight edges. You will probably have to pin the first join and test it by opening out the strip before stitching. Stitch all joins.

Press each join carefully. The flattest effect is achieved by using the toe of the iron and opening the seam. Press on the wrong side and then on the right, then trim both raw edges of the join to 3 mm.

However, many fine fabrics, except knits, will wrinkle when pressed in this way. Avoid it by pressing both turnings to one side, first trimming the upper one to 2 mm. Press on the wrong side and the right side (fig 10.4).

With strip right-side up cut off all extending corners of fabric.

Fig 10.4

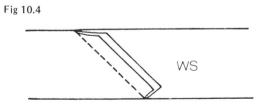

Stretching

Purchased binding has had the excess stretch removed but if you cut your own it should be stretched and pressed to make it easier to handle. Only true cross strips of woven fabric need to be stretched and knit fabric cut on the true cross, others do not 'give' excessively.

Pin one end of the strip to the pressing board, stretch the strip slightly, not to its maximum and pin at the other end of the board. Press with a medium-hot iron and damp muslin. Remove the muslin and leave the strip to cool before moving on to press the next section (fig 10.5).

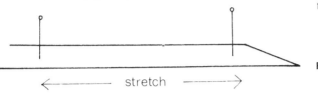

Fig 10.5

FOLDED BIAS FINISH

This edge finish can be of any width from about 1 cm up to 3 cm. It is not suitable for use on an edge that is very shaped. Use matching or contrast fabric.

Where possible, leave one garment seam open, if only at the edge where the bias is to go, rather than attach it to a completed edge. The illustrations below show the bias being attached to a short sleeve but it may also be used wide on a dress hem, or jacket front edges; narrow on a neckline or armhole. If the length is critical, for example on sleeves or a skirt, cut the garment to finished length minus the width of the strip being applied.

Cut pieces twice the finished visible width plus two seam allowances of 5 mm. Fold in half with wrong sides together and press. Place the strip to the right side of the garment with edges arranged so that you can stitch, taking a 5 mm turning on the bias strip but the usual seam allowance on the garment. Insert a few pins across the strip. Machine in place with strip uppermost (fig 10.6). Trim all three raw edges to 3-4 mm and neaten by working zig-zag stitch over them. Press so that the strip extends beyond the garment edge but the turnings lie back into the garment.

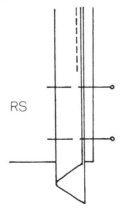

Fig 10.6

Fold the garment, sleeve, etc., right sides together, line up the joins just made and insert a pin to hold in place. Stitch the seam, starting on the join and machining to the hemline. Turn the garment over and complete the seam. Press. Stitching in two stages in this way ensures that the strip is exactly level at the seam (fig 10.7).

Fig 10.7

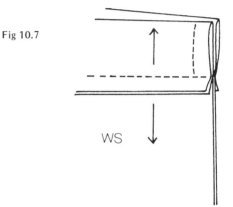

FLAT BIAS FINISH

The bias strip is folded to the right side to be finished and can be almost any width although if there are curves to manipulate keep it to no more than 2 cm. Use to finish any edge including necklines, armholes, edges of jackets, boleros. It is particularly effective when applied to quilted fabric as it provides a contrast in texture. Use matching or contrasting fabric. This finish is only successful with woven binding. The binding can be the final process as the join is not difficult to make. This method does not add to the length.

Cut bias pieces the finished width plus two seam allowances of 5 mm. Join and then press under 5 mm all along one edge.

Begin placing the binding in position at a point where a join will not be visible, for example at the back of the neck, side seam or centre back. If there is a seam the join should fall where the seam comes. Leave an end about 2 cm long for joining.

Place the strip right-side down to wrong side of garment edge. Take 5 mm turning on the bias but the normal seam allowance or whatever is necessary on the garment. If you are skilled at controlling your machine the binding can be stitched on without tacking. Be sure to take an even seam allowance all along, perhaps using the machine foot as a guide. You will find that you tend to slightly pull the bias strip while machining and this produces a good finish. Do not pin or the binding will wrinkle. This process is particularly easy when using a light binding on a

Fig 10.8

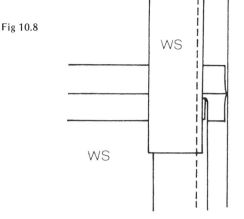

Fig 10.9

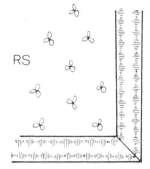

thicker or firmer fabric such as quilting.

On reaching the end, fold over the end of the binding underneath and continue stitching the strip over the fold. The folded edge should be exactly level with the garment seam. Fasten off the stitching. (fig 10.8).

A flatter but more time-consuming join can be made as follows. Begin and end the machining 4 cm away from the ends of binding. Using the iron, press over both ends of binding at an angle so that the folds meet. Lift up these ends and place the pressed creases together. Stitch the join by hand or machine. Trim the raw edges to 3 mm and press. Complete the machining to attach the strip to the garment.

To finish, place the garment wrong-side up on the pressing board. Use the toe of the iron and run it between the garment and the binding, pushing against the join to turn the binding over so that it extends beyond the garment. Trim the garment edge down to 3 mm.

With garment wrong-side towards you roll the binding completely to the right side, roll the edge and tack so that the join is just visible. Press.

Turn to the right side and tack the binding flat to the garment. If you haven't time to tack, pin across the binding at intervals.

Work a straight zig-zag or embroidery stitch along this edge and also along the garment edge if you wish. Press. If the main fabric is printed, match the stitching with one of the colours (fig 10.9).

This finish may also be applied to the right side of the garment and finished on the wrong side. Work the final machine stitching from the right side to make sure it is even.

NARROW BOUND FINISH

This can be applied to any straight or shaped edge such as necklines, sleeve hems, jacket edges. Keep the finish narrow or it may pucker.

The garment is lengthened by the finished width of the binding, so if the length is critical apply it taking a longer seam allowance on the garment. It may be applied before or after seams have been stitched.

Use the narrow purchased binding, plain or printed, or cut strips twice the finished width plus two 5 mm seam allowances. Join and press over one edge with the iron.

Joins should be placed out of sight at the side or back of the garment. Place the binding right-side down to the wrong side of the garment. Take 5 mm seam allowance on the binding but the usual amount (or 5 mm more) on the garment. Machine in place leaving at least 2 cm if a join has to be made. You will slightly stretch the binding as you stitch but this produces a good result.

Make a join by one of the two methods described under *Flat bias finish*.

To finish, use the toe of the iron and run it between the garment and the binding, pushing against the join to press the binding over so that it extends beyond the garment edge (fig 10.10).

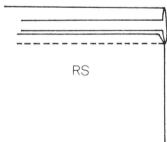

Fig 10.10

Trim the garment edge to 4 mm, or 3 mm if the fabric is thick.

With right side garment towards you, roll the binding over to the right side and tack with the folded edge, just covering the machining beneath.

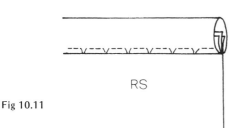

RS

Fig 10.11

Fig 10.12

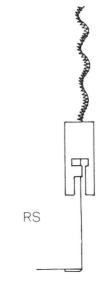

RS

It is not wise to stitch this without tacking.

Press. Work a straight, zig-zag or machine embroidery stitch along the edge of the binding using a matching or contrasting thread.

This finish may be applied to the right side and finished on the wrong side of the garment, in which case finish by hand hemming into the machining or, if machining, work the stitching from the right side for an even result (fig 10.11).

NARROW HEMS

Fluted hem

This is very successful on jersey and knits and also on bias edges of fine fabrics such as chiffon. Use the fluted hem on dresses and skirts, sleeves, scarves, collars, frills.

Cut the garment edge to the required length plus 3-5 mm.

Set the machine to satin stitch of medium width, about 2 to 2½. Place the garment edge under the foot, right-side up, turning under 3-5 mm or as little as possible, depending on the thickness of the fabric. Work two or three machine stitches over the fold to start then satin stitch along the edge. The machine needle must clear the folded edge on the right with every stitch. Stretch the fabric by pulling it at the front as it approaches the needle, and also at the back behind the foot. This opens out the satin stitch to a zig-zag. Pull the fabric as much as possible for the best results (fig 10.12).

After machining the hem, trim off the surplus raw edge of fabric. Use small scissors and cut carefully. The fabric may flute up a little more after removing this edge. Do not press the hem.

Contrasting thread may be used.

Machined-twice hem

This is suitable for any fine woven or jersey fabric and can be used on any garment edge. It produces good results on flared skirts as the two rows of stitching stabilise and add weight.

Trim the garment to the correct length plus 5-6 mm.

Set the machine to a medium-length straight stitch. Work the first row of machining 2 mm inside the raw edge. Feed the fabric into the machine evenly to avoid stretching.

To work the second row place the hem under the machine foot wrong-side up, fold the raw edge over twice forming a very narrow hem. The first row of machining is hidden but it provides a firm edge to grasp, making it easy to roll the hem. Work the second row of machining on the fold (fig 10.13).

Fig 10.13

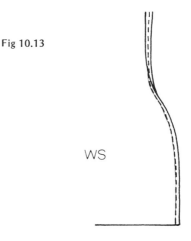

WS

Rolled hem

Use the hemming foot on your machine for this. It is suitable for any fine woven or jersey fabric but work a trial hem on spare fabric just to make sure it is a suitable finish and to practise holding the fabric correctly. Use on any garment edge. It is particularly useful as a time-saver on long edges of frills, over dresses, wedding trains and veils, etc.

Trim the garment to the correct length plus 5 mm. When working on woven fabrics cut the fabric just before hemming, because fraying yarns make the hem untidy and it is difficult to trim them off.

Set the machine to a small- to medium-length straight stitch.

Insert the garment hem wrong-side up and feed the edge into the curl of metal on the foot. Lower the foot and start machining. Hold the fabric edge vertically and hold it taut as it enters the roll. Watch the needle to make sure it is catching the hem down continuously (fig 10.14).

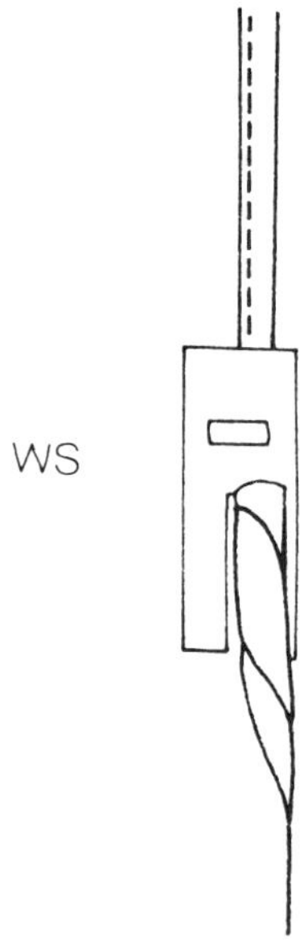

WS

Fig 10.14

Shell hem

This is similar to the rolled hem above and suitable for all light and jersey fabrics. Trim the garment to the correct length plus 5 mm.

Use the shell-hem foot on the machine and a zig-zag stitch, setting about 2½-3 depending on the weight of the fabric. Try the hem out on a spare piece of fabric and adjust the length and width of stitch in order to produce a satisfactory effect.

Insert the garment hem wrong-side up and feed the edge into the curl of the foot. Lower the foot and machine, holding the fabric edge taut and vertical as you feed it in (fig 10.15).

This hem is particularly successful on springy fabrics as the width of the zig-zag holds the edge down well.

Fig 10.15

RS

Ribbon finish

This is an attractive finish on light-weight straight hems. Use on nightwear, lingerie, linings, and also where you are short of fabric for a conventional hem. Use narrow ribbon to match exactly or to contrast.

Trim the garment to the correct length minus two-thirds the width of the ribbon. Set the machine to a small zig-zag stitch.

Place the ribbon right-side up to wrong-side hem, with the edge of the ribbon level with the raw edge of the fabric. Work zig-zag stitch over the edge (fig 10.16).

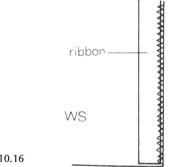

ribbon

WS

Fig 10.16

Using the iron fold this narrow stitched edge over to the right side of the garment so that the ribbon extends beyond the hem edge. The right side of the ribbon now corresponds with the right side of the fabric (fig 10.17).

Fig 10.17

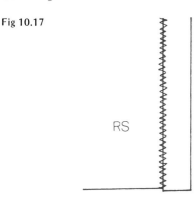

Fig 10.18

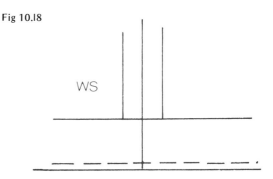

Set the machine to a slightly larger stitch, or better still to an embroidery stitch that will cover the zig-zag underneath, and work the stitch over the edge of the ribbon.

Braid and petersham ribbon can also be used successfully in this way and it can be of any width. Wide ribbon is not successful as it is light in weight and tends to wrinkle.

CONVENTIONAL HEM

This takes longer to do and requires more care but can be used on all except light transparent fabrics. It is the usual method for skirts, dresses and trousers.

If the hemline is straight or only slightly shaped the hem depth can be 5 cm deep. If the skirt is shaped, reduce the depth to 2 or 3 cm in order to avoid the problem of excess fullness in the hem. With circular or very shaped hems the fabric is probably very light in weight so one of the narrow hems described previously will be more suitable.

When using Wundaweb in the hem the depth should be the width of the adhesive plus 5 mm, i.e. 3.5 cm. It is important to keep to this depth which allows sufficient fabric to cover the Wundaweb.

Decide on the length of the garment and mark the fold line with chalk dashes on the right side. Trim the seam allowance of side seams and other seam to 5 mm where the seam falls within the hem, but leave seams at full width in the actual fold of the hem. If too much is trimmed the hem becomes limp and the shape of the hem may be lost.

Fold the garment on the chalk line and tack 3 mm from the folded edge. The stitches should not be too small but they should be even in size at about 3 cm. This row of tacking cannot be omitted (fig 10.18).

Arrange the hem wrong-side up on the pressing surface and press the fold. Make sure you do not allow the iron to rest on the raw edge of the hem. Control it by using the iron sideways to press the fold.

Trim the surplus fabric away so that the hem is a suitable depth. Neaten the raw edge by working a medium-sized zig-zag stitch over the raw edge. It is as well not to omit this even if the fabric does not fray, because the stitching stabilises the edge.

The hem section must now be attached to the garment.

If using Wundaweb, arrange the hem on the pressing surface with wrong side of garment uppermost. Settle a short section of the hem, making sure it is unwrinkled. Slide the Wundaweb between the hem and the garment. Push one edge right down to the tacking, lay the hem edge back in position to completely cover the Wundaweb and press. Use a damp cloth and hot iron and press sharply several times, using the iron sideways and pressing over the hem fold but not on the neatened edge, otherwise an impression of it will show through.

The adhesive web must be completely melted to be effective, so press sharply three or four times in one position and gently lift the hem edge to make sure it has stuck before moving on. Because of the pressure needed, Wundaweb is not suitable for pile fabrics. It is advisable to test it first on others with a surface interest, e.g. crêpe, bouclé and also when using fine transparent fabrics.

When inserting Wundaweb in a curved hem, cut the Wundaweb at intervals and overlap it to make it fit the curve.

Narrower hems can be made, cutting the Wundaweb down the middle but it is only sufficient on a light-weight fabric on a hem that does not need to weight the garment, for example, a frill.

To stitch the hem down, first tack a little below the neatening to hold the hem to the garment.

Thread a small needle with a short piece of matching thread and knot the end. Hold the hem with the lower fold towards you, lift the neatened edge and roll it back towards you and, starting the thread in the fabric of the hem, work catch stitch. Work from right to left picking up one thread from the garment, moving forward 5 mm and taking a couple

Fig 10.19

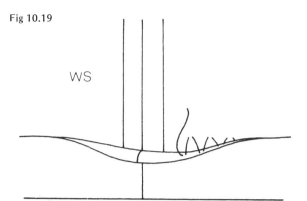

WS

of threads from the hem fabric, move forward, pick one thread from the garment and so on. This is a slow job and it should not be hurried. If the thread is pulled through the garment too quickly it dislodges the weave and can make the hem show (fig 10.19).

Do not pull the thread tight but leave each diagonal of thread fairly loose. Do not try to close the hem fabric tight up against the garment. When sewing on jersey fabric leave an extra loop of thread 1 cm long every 4 cm. This allows for the fabric to stretch in wear but not pull the thread so tight that the hem shows.

Begin and end all lengths of thread in the hem edge, not in the garment.

Remove all tacking and press the hem. Arrange it on the pressing surface wrong-side up and press the hem fold. Use the iron sideways on the fold to ensure that you do not press the stitched edge. Pressing will cause a ridge to show on the right side.

Turn the hem right-side up and press very lightly over the hem and the garment. The hem is quite likely to be the final process so this may be the final pressing of the entire garment.

On medium to heavy fabrics it may be necessary to press more heavily for good results. To do this, arrange the hem wrong-side up and press the fold as described, but then place a piece of spare fabric, folded, up against the hem edge but on the single layer of garment. This fabric will cushion the pressure of the iron and a hem mark will be less likely on the garment. Now press with gentle, not sharp, pressure over the whole hem area.

> TIP Allow a hem to cool and dry before hanging the garment — the weight of the hem fold pulling on the stitches while the fabric is warm and damp may cause stretching but will certainly create a line on the right side.

FRINGE EDGE

Use bought fringing and place it on the right side of the garment edge with the right-side down. Machine in position with a medium-length straight stitch. Stitch close to the edge of the fringe. Press the fabric back away from the fringe. Set the machine to a small zig-zag stitch or a decorative stitch and work it on the right side close to the edge. Trim away the surplus fabric on the underneath (figs 10.20 and 10.21).

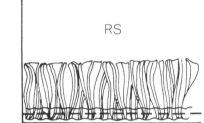

RS

Fig 10.20

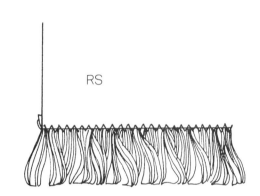

RS

Fig 10.21

CASING EDGE

A casing may be added to an edge to have elastic, cord, etc., threaded through. A casing may be preferable to a hem where there is insufficient fabric to turn up, where the fabric is bulky or where the edge is too shaped to turn a good hem.

Use lining fabric, nylon jersey, fine cotton fabric or the fabric of the garment. Cut bias strips wide enough to contain the elastic or cord plus 1 cm. Join the strips if necessary. Press under one end of the casing.

Place casing strip right-side down on to the right side of the garment taking the correct seam allowance on the garment but only 5 mm on the casing. Machine with a straight stitch. At the end turn over the casing and stitch across it (fig 10.22).

Fig 10.22

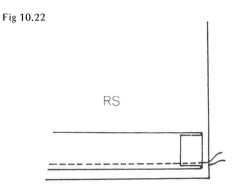

Slide the toe of the iron between the casing and the garment, pushing the casing over until it is right-side up and flat. Turn fabric wrong-side up and roll the casing over; press.

Machine near the edge using a straight, zig-zag or decorative stitch. Turn under the remaining raw edge of the casing and press. Insert pins across the casing to stop it from moving and machine on the fold using the same stitch as on the other edge. Remove the pins as you approach them (fig 10.23).

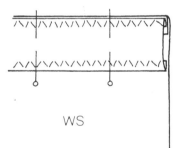

Fig 10.23

11 Facings

Facings are used to neaten shaped edges such as necklines and armholes, to provide a double layer of fabric where buttons and buttonholes are to be used, and also to make certain areas, such as revers, double sided.

Interfacing is often inserted between the facing and the garment so there is the added advantage that the facing covers the interfacing on the inside.

CUTTING THE FACING

The edge to be faced may be shaped, in which case the facing is cut with one edge corresponding in shape. In the case of necklines and armholes the pattern provided will usually be in two pieces. Save time by pinning the pieces together and cutting the facings in one piece as follows.

Necklines

Place the neckline facings together at the shoulder, overlapping the paper if seam allowances are allowed. Pin. Place the new pattern on to the fabric, folded double with the centre back edge on the fold. Cut out (fig 11.1).

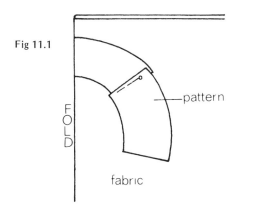

Fig 11.1

If the neckline is to be turned back at the front to form a rever it may look better if the centre front edge of the facing piece is placed on the straight grain to ensure that the grain or pattern matches

the centre front of the garment. If you decide to do this, cut out allowing a seam allowance at the centre back and make a seam (fig 11.2).

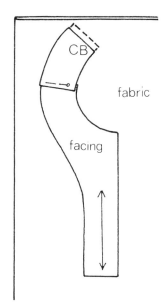

Fig 11.2

> **TIPS** If you fold the fabric wrong-side out you can cut out and stitch the facing join accurately before removing the pattern. Do not neaten the raw edges of the join but do press them open and trim them to 5 mm.
>
> Although cutting the facings by these methods means that the fabric grain does not correspond with the garment grain at every point, this will not affect the handling or wear of the garment. After all, if the fabric is soft or liable to 'give' you will be interfacing it anyway to hold it in place.

Buttoned edge

If the edge to be faced is straight you can save time by cutting it so that it is part of the garment and is simply folded back into position. If the edge is slightly shaped it is usually possible to straighten it without spoiling the design. To do this pin the pattern to paper or light Vilene and draw a straight line, using a felt pen and ruler, joining the two extreme corners of the pattern. This new line will be the fold-over line. Trim off any surplus paper beyond this line.

If the pattern edge is already straight, begin by cutting off the seam allowance if it is there, then pin to paper. Fold back the seam allowance, if there is one, on the facing pattern and pin it to the paper with its long edge against the edge of the piece already in position. Pin.

If the edge is shaped, still fold the paper to a straight edge, drawing a line first if you need it.

Cut out round the outside of this new shape to produce the pattern with fold-back facing. Leave the paper pieces in position to provide the markings, fold line, centre front that you will be transferring to the fabric (fig 11.3).

Fig 11.4

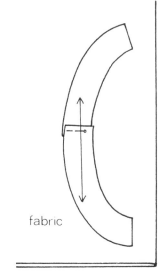

fabric

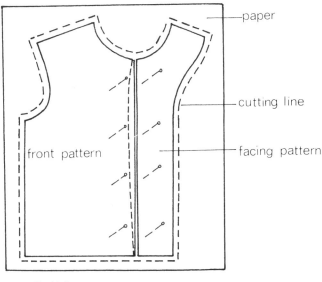

paper

cutting line

front pattern

facing pattern

Fig 11.3

Armholes

If the garment is sleeveless place the two armhole-facing pattern pieces together at the shoulder, overlapping the paper if seam allowances have been provided. Fold the fabric and pin down this new one-piece facing. Arrange it so that the straight grain runs along the part that will face the armhole across the shoulder. Cut out (fig 11.4).

Neck and armholes all-in-one

If the pattern provides separate neck and armhole pieces save time by using instead one facing to cover both areas.

Begin by pinning the neck-facing pattern on top of the dress pattern. Do this with the front and the

back, matching the edges. Pin this assembly to paper or light Vilene. Outline the edge with felt pen following the neckline and any part of the centre front or centre back edge that is covered by the original facing. Outline the entire shoulder edge, the armhole edge and 10-12 cm of the side seam (fig 11.5).

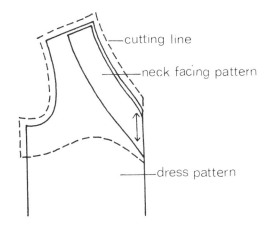

cutting line

neck facing pattern

dress pattern

Fig 11.5

Remove the original pattern and draw a gently curving line across the new pattern from the side seam to join the base of the line you have drawn at the centre front. Mark the straight grain position parallel with the centre front edge and the centre back edge.

Place the pattern pieces on folded fabric with the centre front and centre back to the fold unless there is to be an opening in the garment. Cut out.

Interfacing

Support faced necklines and buttoned openings with interfacing and also those that fold back or are liable to be worn undone, for example zipped at centre front. Do not interface armholes, although a shoulder may be interfaced, see *Interfacing*, chapter 12. Also see that chapter for information on choice of interfacing and methods of attaching.

After cutting out the facings remove the pattern, cut 1 cm from the outer edge of the pattern and pin the remainder to folded interfacing. Cut out. This ensures that the facing will cover the interfacing.

Attach the interfacing pieces to the wrong side of the garment. Stitch garment seams and press. If you are turning the facings to the right side of the garment for decoration attach the interfacing to the right side but stitch the seams in the usual way (fig 11.6).

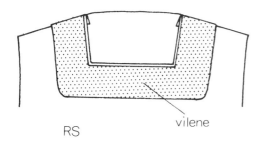

RS   vilene

Fig 11.6

Do not interface an area that is to be gathered. If necessary trim down the facing pattern by more than 5 mm to make it sufficiently narrow to pass beside gathers. If the front neckline is entirely gathered, interface the back neck only.

PREPARING THE FACING

Make the joins. Place the fabric right-sides together and insert one pin some distance from the edge. Machine, remove pin, press open. Trim the raw edges down to 3 mm. Press again.

Neaten the entire outer edge, that is, any cut edge of facing that will not be joined to the garment. Either zig-zag over the edge or if the fabric is fine, place it under the machine right-side up and turning under the raw edge by the smallest possible amount, edge stitch with a straight or small zig-zag stitch. Press the stitching (fig 11.7).

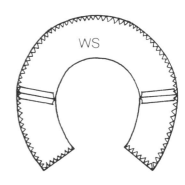

WS

Fig 11.7

ATTACHING THE FACING

Arrange the neck edge on the table right-side up. Place the facing right-side down on top with centre backs matching. Insert one pin near the raw edges at right angles to the edge.

Put one hand under the garment and lift the neckline off the table, bring the ends of the facing round to the centre front (or it may be the back) and pin to the garment (fig 11.8).

Fig 11.8

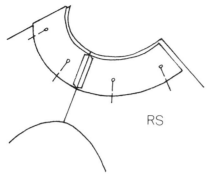

RS

Fig 11.10

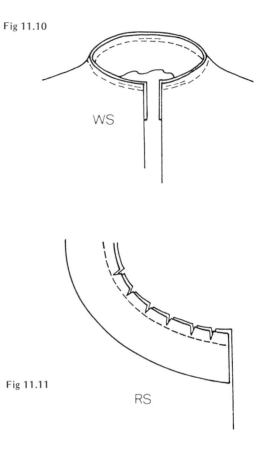

WS

Fig 11.11

RS

Holding the neckline in this position and keeping the raw edges together, insert pins at an angle, well away from the raw edge.

Put the neckline under the machine, and stitch for 2 cm across the centre back, 5 mm in from the edge. Remove the pin just as you lower the foot. Move round to the front and work a short row of stitches at the centre front. This anchors the facing at the vital points (fig 11.9).

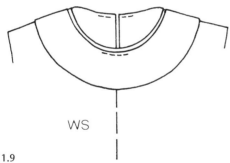

WS

Fig 11.9

Turn the work over so that you have the garment uppermost and stitch by machine right round the neck on the marked seam line or taking 1.5 cm seam allowance.

Remove all pins. Press the stitching flat and then push the toe of the iron under the facing but on top of the garment, and run it round the neck as far as you can. Push the iron forward slightly to turn the facing over so that it is right-side up (fig 11.10).

If you had to turn any corners you will not be able to insert the iron but press up to it on both sides.

Using small scissors, make snips through the raw edges and also the interfacing every 5 mm round all curves. Snip to within a thread of the stitching (fig 11.11).

> **TIP** Angle the snips and you are unlikely to cut through the machine stitching — cutting straight up to a line is dangerous and difficult to control, but if the blades are angled they tend to rest beside the stitching.

Using medium-sized scissors, trim the snipped turnings down to 3 mm and then cut the facing edge down a little further if the fabric is anything but very light weight. At corners cut the surplus away completely, cutting across the corner and then snipping back even further.

FINISHING THE FACING

Hold the garment with the right side towards you, roll the facing over out of sight, hold the edge and roll so that the join is quite exposed, and tack 3 mm from the edge. Press the edge. Turn the garment over so that the facing is uppermost, slip short pieces of Wundaweb between the facing and the garment at intervals of about 5 cm and press well with a hot iron and a damp cloth (fig 11.12).

Fig 11.12

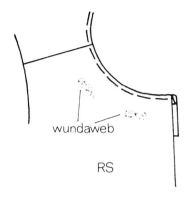

wundaweb

RS

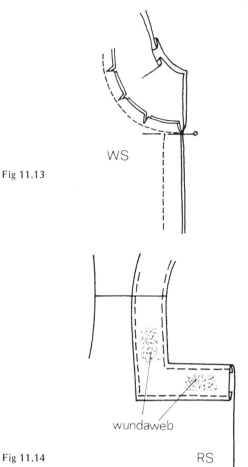

WS

Fig 11.13

Fig 11.14

wundaweb

RS

TIPS When stitching corners, stop and work one machine stitch across the corner. This makes it easier to turn out than a sharp right angle.

Put a small folded piece of Wundaweb on the end of your left thumb when turning corners through. Push your thumb into the corner, roll the facing over and pull the garment right side out. When pressed, the Wundaweb will melt, prevent fraying and slightly stiffen the corner.

When inserting the Wundaweb to hold the finished facing in position, put the first pieces at the centre front and centre back, press to avoid buckling and then place two or three more pieces between these.

Armhole facing

Neaten the facing edge but do not join the ends. Stitch and press garment shoulder seams only. Attach the armhole facing and snip and trim the turnings. Fold the garment right-sides together, matching the side seams and insert one pin across this seam exactly on the facing and armhole join. Stitch the seam from armhole to hem. Remove the pin, turn the garment over and complete the stitching across the facing. Press open the seam. Trim the turnings within the facing to 3 mm and neaten the seam (fig 11.13).

TIP If you find it difficult to establish the angle at which to machine across the facing in order to ensure that it lies flat when turned down inside the garment, press open and neaten the remainder of the seam, roll the armhole facing to the wrong side and tack and press the edge, at the same time pressing the two ends of facing. The folds of facing should meet. Finish by slip stitching by hand.

Decorative facing

Do not neaten the outer edge of the facing. Attach to the wrong side, trim, snip, roll tack and press the edge. Set your adjustable marker to the width at which you wish to finish the facing, hold it in your left hand and turn under the raw edge of the facing level with the marker. Tack the edge as you fold. Press the edge. While at the ironing surface, slip pieces of Wundaweb under the facing and press (fig 11.14).

Finish by working a machine stitch, straight, zig-zag or embroidery.

TIP If the facing has a shaped or decorative outer edge, do not cut it to shape when cutting out. Cut a straight outer edge but mark with tailor tacks or carbon paper the shaped outer edge. After attaching the facing, turn in and tack on this marked line, snipping away the surplus fabric as you go.

Combined neck and armhole facing

Place the back and front facings with right sides together and join the shoulder and under-arm seams. Press open and trim the edges down to 3 mm. Arrange the facing round the neck of the garment, pinning and stitching as described previously and trimming and tacking the edge too. The facing is now completely on the wrong side of the garment (fig 11.15).

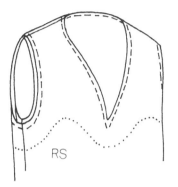

Fig 11.15

With the right side of the garment outwards, turn in the armhole edge and tack close to the fold. The edge will spring up again, so snip it almost to the fold. Trim the raw edge down to 5 mm and press the folded edge.

Still with the right side outwards spread the facing out underneath until it is in the correct position, armhole edges matching. Insert pins, at an angle, round the armhole, well within the edge. Turn the garment wrong side out, insert pieces of Wundaweb between the facing and the garment. Start by putting one piece at the shoulder area and another at the under-arm then space two more on each side between these two. The Wundaweb should not be too close to the armhole edge (fig 11.16).

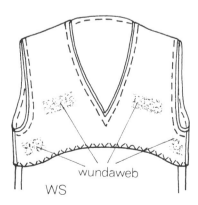

Fig 11.16

Trim the facing edge until it extends beyond the garment edge by only 3 mm. Snip this edge every 1 cm.

With the facing side towards you, turn in this raw edge and tack it to the garment with the edge 1 mm back from the armhole. Press.

Finish by slip-stitching round the armhole, or by machining. Use edge stitching, a zig-zag stitch or a decorative stitch (fig 11.17).

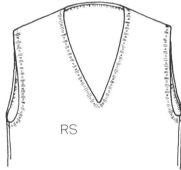

Fig 11.17

12 Interfacing

WHAT, WHY AND WHERE?

The answer to why is that interfacing adds crispness and form to those parts of the garment where it is applied. This not only strengthens those areas but also ensures that the garment continues to look good while worn.

What to use for interfacing depends on the fabric and style of the garment. Some places may need heavy reinforcement, e.g. waistbands and shirt collars, while some may only require the lightness of adhesive web to provide extra body.

Where to interface? The following list is a general guide but of course you wouldn't always interface all these areas. You must select the interfacing for the area according to the particular fabric and style. Any part that will be handled in wear must be interfaced, plus any style features.

1 All collars	Stand collars – medium or firm
	Roll collars – soft or medium
2 Cuffs	Wide cuffs – firm
	Narrow bands – medium
3 Dress yokes	Soft or light
4 Skirt or trouser yokes	Soft or light
5 Waistbands	Very firm or medium
6 Belts	Very firm, medium or soft
7 Neckbands	Soft or medium
8 Strap neckline openings	Soft or medium
9 Patch and seam pockets	Soft or light
10 Pocket welts and flaps	Medium or firm
11 Necklines and shoulders – no collars	Soft or light
12 Piped buttonholes	Soft or light
13 Fastening areas	Soft or light
14 Weak points – slits, etc.	Light
15 Hems	Light
16 Pleats	Light

TYPES OF INTERFACING

There are light, soft, medium and firm interfacings that can be sewn in and a similar choice of the type that is ironed in place. These are sold by the metre about 82 cm wide or in pre-packs containing one piece. Both types have to be cut to shape.

There are packs of a pre-cut strip, one is soft and iron-on, the other an adhesive web. There is also an adhesive web with paper backing (torn away after pressing in place) in packets containing a sheet which you cut to shape. There is a wide variety of belt stiffenings and petershams of varying widths, some in pre-packs, some sold by the metre. These are referred to in detail in the section on waist finishes.

All the iron-on and adhesive interfacings are quick to use because sewing is eliminated, but be sure you are using ones that are suitable for your fabric. Try out a small piece on a scrap of fabric if in doubt.

Vilene is the most widely available interfacing in the biggest range. There is something suitable for every fabric and every process. The chart on the following page is the entire range at present and I have indicated which will produce the results listed as desirable in the chart on this page.

HOW TO INTERFACE

Attach the interfacing to the garment piece itself on the wrong side of the fabric. Never interface a facing: it makes it stand away from the garment; it becomes too important compared with the garment; it does nothing to support the garment; it does not reinforce the piece of fabric taking the strain of wear because facings take no strain. Attaching interfacing to the facing is a technique employed in making ready-to-wear clothes because it is quicker and requires little accuracy, but it is not a technique that we should copy. Many people complain that neck and armhole facings, and front facings of a ready-made blouse, dress, etc., pop out, and this is solely because they are interfaced.

The principle is the same for collars and cuffs: it is the piece which is part of the garment that is interfaced, i.e. the outer cuff (or the whole cuff), the

Types of interfacing

Vilene	Area	Which fabrics	Result
Ultrasoft light – white and charcoal	Collars, cuffs, yokes, tie belts, neckbands, patch and seam pockets, neck and shoulder fastening areas, collars, cuffs, openings	Medium and light including velveteen, wools, silk, cotton, fine, including silks, voile, georgette	Soft
Ultrasoft medium	Collars, cuffs, pocket flaps, openings, shoulders, yokes	Medium, including wool, linen	Slightly crisp
Medium iron-on	Collars, cuffs	Firm, including cotton and woven synthetics	Medium firm
Firm iron-on	Belts, waistbands, pocket flaps	Firm	Very firm
Super stretch	Collars, cuffs, yokes	All knits and soft fabrics with give	Soft
Light sew-in – white and charcoal	Collars, cuffs, openings, yokes, stand collars, bands, cuffs, pocket flaps	All fine and medium	Soft
Medium sew-in	Stand collars, bands, cuffs, pocket flaps, openings	Medium weight	Firm
Heavy sew-in	Belts, waistbands	Any	Very firm
Soft Fold-a-Band	Pleats, hems, turn-back cuffs, openings, straps, cuffs, bands	All except very fine and pile fabrics	Medium
Heavy Fold-a-Band	Belts, welts, waistbands		
Wundaweb	Hems, openings, fraying areas, buttonholes	All except very fine or transparent and pile fabrics	Slightly crisp but fine
Bondaweb	Buttonhole pipings, openings, appliqué, fraying areas	All except pile fabrics	Soft

under collar, the piece attached to the neckline that is outermost when the collar is standing up and not folded into a style. The exceptions are when using Fold-a-Band and Wundaweb. They are strips and are therefore attached equally to garment and facing.

Interfacing is a very important step in construction and one not to be skimped. The quickest way to do it is to use iron-on methods.

If the result is unsatisfactory it means you have used the wrong weight of interfacing; the most common fault is using one that is too stiff for the fabric. Choose the one that is most like your fabric then it will be easy to handle. Problems nearly always occur if you have an area that is far stiffer than the remainder of the garment. The secret of successful interfacing is that it should be impossible to detect it by looking at the outside of the finished garment.

Iron-on interfacing

Attach before beginning to construct the garment.

Fold a sheet of dressmaker's carbon paper with the right side out and slip it between the layers of a folded piece of Vilene (fold it with shiny or adhesive side outside).

If the interfacing shape is to correspond with a pattern shape such as cuff, collar, pocket, yoke or front edge, place the pattern on the Vilene, using the fold if the pattern requires it.

Using a tracing wheel mark round the outer edges of the pattern. Where you are cutting interfacing for a buttoned opening, mark the neck and part of the shoulder, run the wheel down the centre front line but mark the cutting edge 1-2 cm beyond this. At the outer edge mark a cutting line on the Vilene 2 cm narrower than the garment facing. This ensures that the Vilene extends beyond the centre front line and folds back making a better edge to the garment, and it ensures that the interfacing will be covered by the facing on the inside.

Remove the paper pattern and cut the Vilene. On outside edges cut 2-3 mm within the dotted line. This ensures that the Vilene is smaller than the fabric piece and so the adhesive will not stick to the ironing surface.

Place all fabric to be interfaced with wrong side up, place Vilene pieces with the adhesive side down and insert a pin towards one side of the piece. Carry to the pressing board, press up to the pin, remove the pin, press the other half in position (fig 12.1).

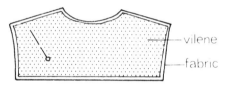

Fig 12.1

Hold the iron in position for a couple of seconds before moving it. Press all parts several times with a steady plonking movement. Do not slide the iron. Use a damp cloth when attaching Softline. Allow the pieces to cool.

Strip interfacing

Mainly used during construction or to complete a process.

When using Wundaweb press a fold, or tack and press, cut a piece of Wundaweb slightly longer than needed and place it carefully between the layers of fabric.

Make sure the edge goes right to the tacking or into the folded edge; if it has to reach into a corner tuck it well in, folding the surplus Wundaweb over. When using several strips, cut to length, cutting lengthways too if necessary, put all pieces in position and smooth out the top fabric. When putting Wundaweb into a small unbroken hem such as trousers or sleeves, insert the whole length of Wundaweb and

pull the fabric of the hem, tugging it to make it lie flat. This prevents the fabric from wrinkling (fig 12.2).

Fig 12.2

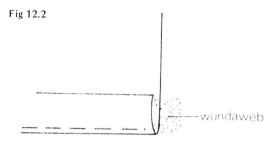

Use a damp cloth and a hot iron, press with steady plonking movements and press three or four times on each area. Make sure the adhesive web has thoroughly melted. It helps when pressing a large area to go along it a second time after allowing a few moments to cool; it is then easier to detect the unstuck areas.

Do not attempt to hurry, or you will have to do it again. When you think you have pressed sufficiently, turn the garment right-side up and press again, but lightly.

To use Fold-a-Band, press a crease in the fabric if there is to be a fold, e.g. pleat, slit, turn-back cuff, pocket top. Place Fold-a-Bond on WS of fabric, align perforation with the crease and press.

When using it at the start of a process, e.g. cuff or waistband, cut the Fold-a-Band to length and place it on the wrong side of a piece of fabric, matching the perforations to the straight grain, press in position and cut out the fabric using the edge of the Fold-a-Band as a guide but adding seam allowances (fig 12.3).

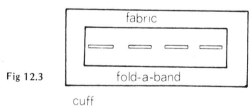

Fig 12.3

cuff

If using it to make an opening such as centre front or neck slit make sure there is a straight line marked on the wrong side of the fabric as a guide. Use tailor's chalk and a ruler or carbon paper.

Place the Fold-a-Band with the adhesive side down to the wrong side of the fabric, aligning the oblong perforations with the crease or marked line. Use a medium-hot iron. Press one side of the interfacing in position, then the second side.

If the full width is not needed press the first side in position then trim down the second side before pressing that too.

To use Bondaweb cut to size and shape and press in position on the wrong side of the fabric. Use a medium-hot iron and damp cloth. Press well with a firm plonking movement until the paper appears mottled. Remove the cloth and allow the fabric to cool: leave it for at least 10 minutes. Lift one corner of the paper and peel it off. Continue sewing, complete buttonholes, opening, etc., then when the Bondaweb has been covered with fabric, press again and it will stick.

Sew-in interfacing

Cut in the same way as for iron-on pieces but it is not necessary to reduce the size of the pieces.

Arrange all fabric pieces to be interfaced with wrong side up. Place interfacing on top and attach to fabric with basting. Start with a knot, make the stitches about 3 cm long. There is no need to fasten off the thread ends (fig 12.4).

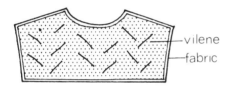

Fig 12.4

Work on the garment and on completion remove the basting stitches.

If the interfacing is very heavy, as on waistbands, it should be cut to size excluding turnings, and the edge attached to the seam allowance of the fabric using herringbone stitch or a machine stitch, or even a strip of Wundaweb.

TIPS Where there is a dart, interface the area, stitch the dart then cut away the interfacing close to the stitching before pressing the dart. If the fabric is bulky, split the entire dart including the fabric, trim away the interfacing and press the dart open (fig 12.5).

Where interfacing extends to a gathered area, shape the interfacing to avoid the gathering, reducing its width to as little as 2-3 cm if necessary (fig 12.6).

If a complete area is to be tucked, e.g. yoke, interface first with the lightest weight iron-on interfacing.

Fig 12.5

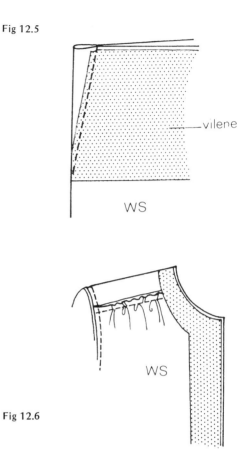

Fig 12.6

GENERAL RULES

When interfacing large areas or those to be folded, e.g. roll or fold collars, openings, yokes, patch pockets, use soft or light interfacing.

When interfacing small, flat unfolded sections, e.g. stand collars, cuffs, bands, pocket flaps, straps, belts, waistbands, use firmer interfacing if a stiffer result if wanted.

In edges such as pleats, hems, slit openings and for reinforcing weak points, use adhesive such as Wundaweb or Bondaweb, and for an accurate straight line or fold use Fold-a-Band.

When stitching matching corners or curves mark the pairs of stitching lines with pencil dots for accuracy.

13 Appliqué

Attach the motif as early as possible in construction while the fabric is still flat. If its position has to be carefully decided then partly make up the garment and add the appliqué before side seams are completed.

Decide on the design. Keep the outline as simple as possible with very few additional rows of stitching that will require careful finishing of threads at the end. Most outlines can be simplified, even initials. Trace the motif shown here, or draw your own design on soft sew-in Vilene and cut out. Pin this to the garment and adjust it until it looks right. Unpin the Vilene but mark its position on the garment with a chalk cross (figs 13.1 and 13.2).

Decide on the fabric for the motif. It does not have to contain the same fibres but it should be washable and of a colour that will not run. The piece can easily be washed before use to test this and to pre-shrink it. Remember that contrasting textures are particularly attractive, for example satin on towelling, and so are contrasting prints and colours.

Decide on the thread colour. This can match either of the fabrics or you can introduce a new colour. Use Anchor Machine Embroidery No. 30 or 50, or, for a heavier result, use normal sewing thread such as Drima.

Set the machine to satin stitch. Stitch length: ¾.

Fig 13.1

Fig 13.2

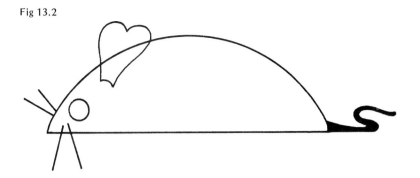

Zig-zag: 1½. Attach the satin stitch foot.

Pin the Vilene template to the fabric and mark round it with a dotted pencil line. Trim away some of the surplus fabric but leave at least 2 cm extending beyond the pencil line. Place the fabric on the right side of the garment. Slip a piece of Wundaweb between the two and press until it adheres.

Put paper underneath and work satin stitch round the design following the line. Try to start and finish at a point convenient for fastening off or for moving on to the next part of the design. If the design has two sections that will partly overlap, work on the underneath one first but avoid a ridge by satin stitching only round that part that will not be covered by the upper part (fig 13.3).

> **TIP** Slip a thin piece of polyester wadding, ½ cm smaller all round than the design, underneath the fabric. Use two pieces of Wundaweb to keep it in position. The resulting appliqué will be slightly padded.

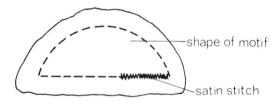

Fig 13.3

Remove the garment from the machine. Tear off the paper. Trim the thread ends and carefully trim away the excess fabric close to the satin stitch. Adjust the stitch to work a zig-zag width of 2, still keeping to a stitch length of ¾. Work round the motif again, stitching exactly over the first row. The slightly wider stitch will cover the first stitching. Remember to put a fresh piece of paper underneath (fig 13.4).

Fig 13.4

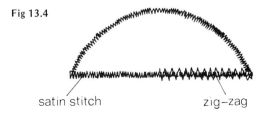

satin stitch   zig-zag

14 Equipment

BASIC TOOLS

You have probably already got at least some of these basic items of equipment, but if you are buying new ones, note the special points to help you choose.

Pins The long ones with coloured plastic heads are easy to pick up and clearly visible.

Tape measure The types marked off in 10 cm sections of different colours are quick to read.

Needles Have packets of Betweens in assorted sizes.

Tailor's chalk Wax squares are less likely to break. Keep edges sharpened.

Adjustable marker (A short metal rule with movable red arrow.) An invaluable tool, much quicker to use than a tape.

Chalk pencil (A white pencil with a brush on the end.) Useful for marking points on fabric.

Pin-holder The magnetic tube holder is spill-proof. It has a piece of Velcro attached and can be used on the wrist or fixed to a surface.

Beeswax One cake will last for years. Essential for waxing thread when sewing on buttons, useful for smoothing out double thread that snarls.

Bodkin (Now made in plastic.) Invaluable for speeding up the removal of tacking threads.

Rouleau turner (Long metal needle with a large eye at one end and a knot at the other.) The only way to turn thin tubing successfully but also useful for turning belts and ties.

Elastic threader (A short, flat metal needle with a large eye.) The most efficient way of threading elastic because it passes easily through casing and will bend to go round curves.

Hem marker The most accurate way of marking a level hemline on a skirt if you have someone on hand at the right moment to use it. The best ones have a heavy metal base and firm upright. The container holding the powdered chalk is moved to the level of what will be the bottom of the skirt. The marks should be made every 10 cm or so, with you moving gently round on one spot. You do not turn up the fabric for marking.

Thread snips (Small scissor-like blades for snapping threads, not fabric.) Very useful by your machine.

Tracing wheel (A spiked wheel with a handle.) The type with a long handle is more comfortable to use than the miniature one. When pushed along dressmaker's carbon paper it transfers pattern markings to fabric.

Use the paper in narrow strips folded double with the carbon side out, slip this between two layers of fabric — right side out — and run the wheel over the paper pattern. The most useful colour paper is orange as it is visible on most fabrics yet does not show through to the right

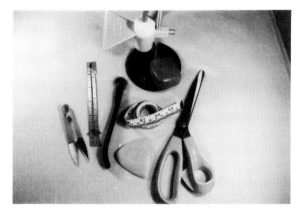

side as dark colours tend to do.

Never mark the right side of the fabric with carbon paper as it often proves impossible to get out.

Small and medium scissors It is always quicker to use the correct tool and it is easier to pick up and use the right size scissors for the job than struggle slowly with the wrong ones.

Cutting out shears Expensive but worth the saving in time and frustration to invest in a really big pair. They are faster and more accurate and much more comfortable to hold.

Thimble A thimble is vital. Trying to sew without one is slow and painful. Use one correctly and hand sewing becomes quick, even and pleasurable. The only type that is completely comfortable and goes unnoticed in wear, so you can keep it on all the time you are sewing, is a tailor's thimble.

OTHER ESSENTIALS

Apart from equipment that you keep ready for use, each time you make something you will buy fabric, thread and other items such as zips. But sewing is easier and much quicker if you have access to some other items that you can choose from and use if appropriate. It helps to build up stocks of these things.

Wundaweb Not only for hems: small pieces hold down facings, etc.

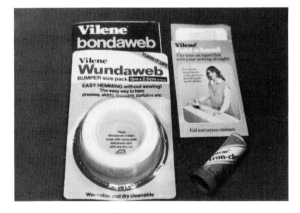

Bondaweb For quick application of motifs, etc., also in small areas to prevent fraying.

Velcro Cut to size and shape for fastenings in any position on any garment.

Elastic petersham Comfortable, useful as a waist stay. An aid to quick fitting.

Trouser clips Large clips for waistbands. Quicker to sew on than two small hooks.

Fold-a-Band Iron-on tape cut to an accurate width with centre marking. Saves hours of measuring in cuffs, bands, straps, belts.

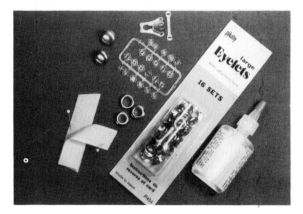

Trims Metal button moulds you cover with fabric. Special press studs are sewn under them.

Studs Metal-capped studs, decorative and quick to apply. Useful in all positions.

Shirring elastic Keep both black and white. Two or three rows of shirring are as effective as one piece of narrow elastic, but more decorative.

Iron-on binding In limited colours, but useful for decorative repairs.

Eyelets The quickest fastening — eyelets and a piece of cord.

Ribbons and narrow petersham ribbon Useful for skirt loops, as a stay in jersey seams and for decoration.

Plastic press studs Transparent, so they are practically invisible, but because they are square they are easy to hold while sewing on.

Fray-Check Keep handy to drop one spot on badly fraying fabrics while handling a process.

PART TWO
The designs

Introduction

The designs in this book have been carefully worked out so that they are quick to make, and as far as possible they avoid the time-consuming processes and activities such as buttonholes, collars and fitting. They have been arranged in order of simplicity — most people will find the early designs take less time to make than those towards the end.

THE PATTERNS

The pattern shapes have been simplified as much as possible without loss of style so that in some cases you can draw the outline with tailor's chalk directly on to the fabric. The measurements are indicated and there are instructions on altering the size if necessary. Although simple in shape, most of the designs are variable. They can all be shortened or lengthened, pockets can be added or omitted, ready-made decoration such as braid or piping can be added if you wish. Many people stick rigidly to a pattern, thinking it will be ruined if they don't. A few variations are suggested with each design. Try them. Try a few ideas of your own as well.

The advantage of diagram-patterns is that you can see all the pattern pieces and their relative shapes at once. It is a good way of learning construction and seeing the way pieces fit together, without having to rely on numbered points — it is obvious when looking at these small-scale diagrams which is the neckline, shoulder, armhole, side seam, etc.

A disadvantage of some diagram-patterns is that they take time to copy. Often they appear so mathematically confusing that the dressmaker doesn't know how or where to start and may well be ex-

hausted before starting to actually sew.

To help to overcome this problem I have described how to draw each pattern, suggesting where to begin, describing the shape of a curve and so on. Also, where a pattern shape is symmetrical I suggest folding a piece of paper and then drawing half the pattern. When cut it becomes the entire piece. This is not only much more accurate, it is very quick.

The grid

It is possible to rule 5 cm squares on a large sheet of plain paper to make a grid, but it is extremely tedious and may not be entirely accurate. It is obviously much better to buy squared pattern paper or, the alternative is to use a cutting board. It has various markings, including 5 cm squares.

For drawing the actual patterns, pin pieces of Light Sew-In Vilene on top of the grid. You can easily see the lines and it keeps the squared paper unmarked. The Vilene makes a good durable pattern. You could, of course, use sheets of tissue or other plain paper as an alternative.

Copying the pattern

The following hints make the job much easier:

Cut the Vilene or paper to size before starting to draw the pattern. It helps when locating points measured in from the edge; the pieces are easier to handle; and you will feel more confident to be working within the confines of a specific area which you know is to be filled.

Use fine felt-tipped pens on Vilene but do not draw continuous lines — they fade and also wrinkle the Vilene. Use a dotted or dashed line even when drawing with a ruler.

Do not try to draw solid lines at curves — that is easy only for draughtsmen. Draw a dotted or dashed line in a sweeping curve.

Never worry about a slight wobble in any line, it is easily corrected when you cut out the pattern piece.

Never add extra 'just in case'. Look at the measurements given and check before you start. The easiest way to check a length measurement is to measure an existing garment. To adjust the patterns in this book, draw in the line as it is given and then draw another line representing the adjustment. If you are enlarging a pattern and the piece of Vilene or paper is not big enough make a note at the pattern edge to add when you are cutting out the fabric.

Use a ruler for straight lines. Even curves are easier to draw if there is a straight line there as a guide. If you haven't a long ruler use a piece of wood — a piece of dowel or thin batten.

Always draw the arrow representing the straight grain.

Always mark 'place to fold' where appropriate.

Always put 'cut two' etc., to remind you when cutting out.

Always write the size on each piece and after use fold up all the pattern pieces together, put a pin through them to hold, and on the outside draw a sketch of the garment — easier to identify than a description.

Caftan

A loose, ankle-length caftan to wear as a robe, holiday cover-up or casual evening dress. It has a slit neck, bound and tied, and two rows of vertical stitching to form side seams.

If the border fabric suggested is used there is only the hem to do in addition to the neck.

Very quick to make — one piece of fabric and takes as little as an hour.

Size: Fits any size up to 150 cm hip

Length: 120 cm from base of front neck slit to hem

Fabric: 3 m. 115 cm border print fabric. If narrow fabric is used buy 6 m of 90 cm fabric and join at the centre front and centre back making a piece of fabric 180 cm wide. After stitching the side seams, trim so that sleeve is correct length. 1 m binding or crossway fabric.

Haberdashery: 1 reel Drima
                   Wundaweb

The pattern: There is no need to make a pattern for this caftan; cut out in fabric.

Cutting out: Fold the fabric right-side out with the folded end and selvedges level. Insert a couple of pins at the centre of the fold and draw a chalk line at right angles to it 25 cm long. Make a small snip at the fold and cut the top layer of fabric only. The first 8 cm of the cut represents the back neck, the remainder is the front neck (fig 1).

From the slit, measure 37 cm out towards the selvedges on each side. Draw a vertical chalk line from there to the raw edges of the fabric. Mark off a point 30 cm from the fold down each line. At the hem measure up 40 cm on each line and mark a point.

Making up: Insert a few pins diagonally across the chalk lines. Stitch on the chalk fastening off the thread at the start and finish of each row. The space between the stitching and the fold forms the armhole. Bind the neck slit, making the join at the 8 cm point so that it does not show. To add ties cut the remainder of the binding in two, stitch, neaten one end of each piece and either insert the raw ends under the neck binding before stitching, or fold under and hem to the wrong side after completing the binding (fig 2).

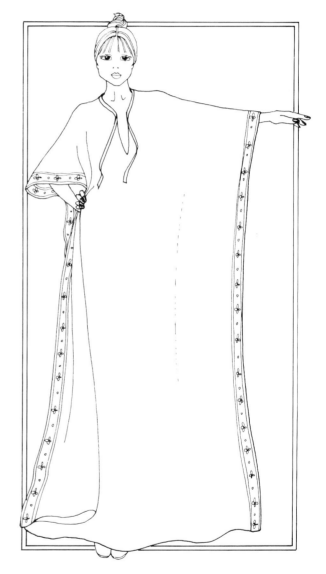

Turn up the hem at the back and front of the caftan, securing with Wundaweb.

Variations: Trim away the four corners at the hem and turn a narrow machined hem on the back and the front.

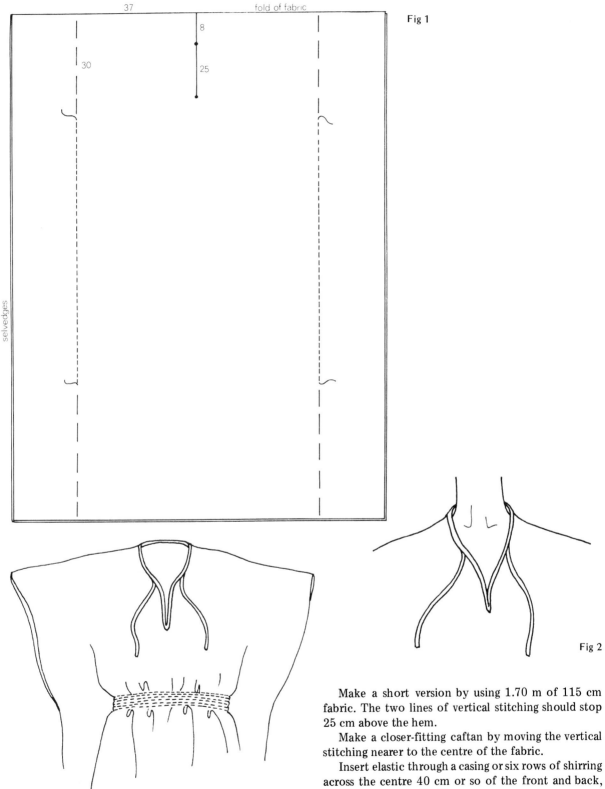

37   fold of fabric

Fig 1

8

30   25

selvedges

Fig 2

Fig 3

Make a short version by using 1.70 m of 115 cm fabric. The two lines of vertical stitching should stop 25 cm above the hem.

Make a closer-fitting caftan by moving the vertical stitching nearer to the centre of the fabric.

Insert elastic through a casing or six rows of shirring across the centre 40 cm or so of the front and back, on your waistline (fig 3).

Wrap

A simple jersey cover-up in plain or print, knotted at the front or side. Make it in towelling and it can be worn after swimming and for changing. Men can use it too. Buy an extra 60 cm of fabric and you can make a matching bikini.

The wrap can be made in only the time it takes to machine the edges — as little as half an hour.

Size: Up to 102 cm hips

Length: 107 cm

Fabric: 1.10 m jersey, knit, velour, stretch towelling

Haberdashery: 1 reel Drima
                    Wundaweb

The pattern: The wrap consists of one piece of fabric so there is no need to cut a pattern.

Cutting out: Fold the fabric down the centre with

Fig 1

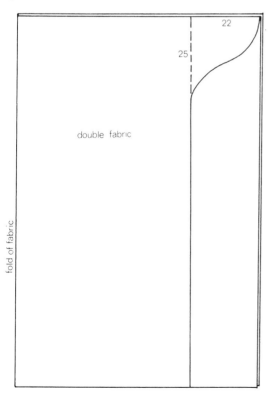

double fabric

right sides out. Make sure the two cut ends are trimmed level. Measure in 22 cm and down 25 cm from the corner. Draw a curve using tailor's chalk, making it convex for half its length and concave below that. A plastic curve may be of help.

From the base of the curve draw a chalk line to the bottom of the fabric, parallel with the selvedges (fig 1).

Cut the double fabric on the chalk line.

Making up: Turn narrow machined hems on both the vertical edges.

Turn narrow machined hems at the top and bottom of the wrap.

Variations: Make double from two layers of contrasting fabric.

Make shorter for a briefer cover-up.

Tie bikini

Bra top and pants made in double fabric and adjusted to size and fastened with cord or rouleau. Can be worn under the Caftan (p. 105) or the Wrap (p. 107).

Quick to make if using purchased cord, otherwise it takes a little longer.

Size: 12-14. Adjust to smaller or one size larger by subtracting or adding small amounts. Adjust the pants at the centre of each pattern piece. Adjust the top along the straight edge that forms the side. If in doubt about adjusting the pattern measure an existing bikini or cut out as shown and fit before stitching.

Seam allowances: 1.5 cm
2 cm at sides of pants

Fabric: 60 cm of jersey, knit, velour, stretch towelling

Haberdashery: 1 reel Drima
4 m cord
3 m narrow elastic

The pattern: Make a pattern by following the diagrams. Half the pants, back and front is shown for ease of drawing. If you fold the paper first, copy the pattern and cut it out, then when opened out you have a full-size pattern. For the front use paper 30 cm deep and 20 cm wide when folded. For the back it should be 30 cm deep and 23 cm wide when folded.

The crutch seam is slightly curved, the waist edge and sides are straight. The leg curve on the front is concave but on the back is almost straight. The latter is easy to draw if you put in a straight line first (fig 1).

The bra cup has a curved edge under the bust, a sloping edge at the side and the edge with greater slope runs from centre front between busts up to the point where ties are attached. It will help if you cut the paper to size first, 22 x 27 cm. Make two copies of the bra section.

Cutting out: Fold fabric on straight grain with wrong side out. Place front and back pants' pattern one below the other, matching the straight grain arrow to the line of knitting on the fabric. Place both bra pattern pieces in position one above the other, with straight grain correctly positioned.

Pin and cut out.

Making up pants: Place back and front together and join the short crutch seam. Make the lining pieces to

Fig 1

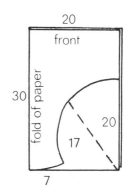

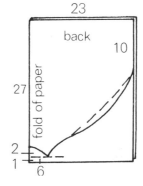

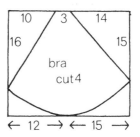

match and place both right sides together. Machine the curves of the legs, trim and turn pants right-side out. Tack along raw edges through both layers to hold. Turn a double hem along the tops of the pants 3 mm wider than the elastic and machine. Machine round both leg curves the same distance from the edge as on the top edge (fig 2).

Fig 2

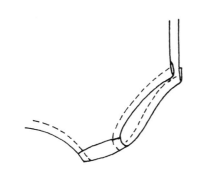

Cut two pieces of elastic 52 cm long and insert one in each leg casing.

Cut two pieces 37 cm long and insert in the upper edges. Adjust length if necessary.

Secure all ends in the casings with double machining. Turn a double hem 2 cm wide on each of the four sides of the pants and machine. Slot 60 cm cord through each tie (fig 3).

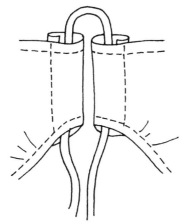

Fig 3

Making up bra: Insert the end of a 60 cm piece of cord at the top corner of one pair of fabric pieces.

Place fabric pieces together in pairs, right sides together. Stitch all round. Take 5 mm seam allowance on the curved edge leaving a 5 cm gap in one straight edge. Trim edges, turn right side out, Slip stitch the gap (fig 4).

Fig 4

Machine along the two straight edges of the triangles just far enough inside the edge to allow the elastic to pass through (the same distance as on the pants). Thread elastic, pulling up the fabric until it is slightly gathered (check this by trying it on) and secure the ends with machining (fig 5).

Fig 5

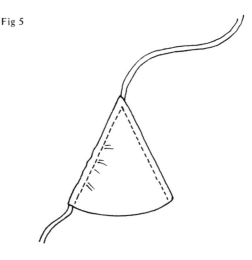

Turn up the lower edges of the triangles and machine sufficient distance from the edge to allow the cord to pass through. Cut a piece of cord 160 cm long and thread it through the lower edges (fig 6).

Fig 6

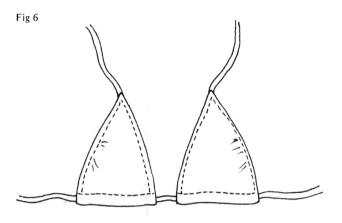

Variations: Make the bikini lining in contrasting fabric. Both the colour and also the texture can be varied.

For more support put the bra triangles on to reversed curved petersham. Make the two bra pieces and insert elastic. Insert a gathering thread along the curved edge of each triangle and pull up a little (try on and adjust). Attach curved petersham to fabric. Attach it to the bra sections with centre front corners meeting. Try on and adjust length of petersham allowing at least 7 cm for an overlapping fastening or 2 cm if a metal clasp is to be used. Complete the petersham band as for a waistband. Attach fastener.

TIP Knot the ends of the cord or attach small wool bobbles to prevent them from pulling out.

Single-seam skirt

Full, long skirt made from one piece of fabric. Easy to make and the perfect choice for border fabrics, stylised prints, awkward geometrics and diagonal designs. Although there are no side seams, there are pockets. The waist is finished with wide elastic in a casing. Could be made in a couple of hours.

Can be worn with the Tie Bikini (p. 109) any version of the Sweater (p. 128) or with the Robe cardigan or waistcoat version (p. 123).

Size: Up to 100-105 cm hip, waist adjustable

Length: 100 cm waist to ankle, can be adjusted to fit or according to the border on the fabric.

Seam allowance: 1.5 cm

5 cm at hem or according to print

Fabric: 2.10 m of 115 cm fabric (the usual width for border design) or

1.80 m of 140 cm fabric or
1.80 m of 150 cm fabric

Haberdashery: 2 reels Drima
Small piece of iron-on Vilene, e.g. Softline for pockets. 35 cm wide x 30 cm deep.
Waist length of wide elastic or elastic petersham
Wundaweb

The pattern: The skirt is a very simple shape that can be cut out in fabric without a pattern.

Cutting out: Straighten the fabric edges and fold the piece in half across the width with the wrong side out. Measure up from the double selvedge 110 cm or whatever length is correct for you. You may have to vary this amount depending on the border and on the width of the unprinted edge at the selvedge. Trim off surplus fabric at the opposite selvedge if necessary. Measure along this the waist edge and find the half-way point. Mark off 4 cm on either side of this point. Measure 45 cm down and rule straight chalk lines from the points at the top edge to this point. From the base of this dart shape, measure straight down for a further 25 cm. Mark this point on the wrong side of the fabric on the upper and under layer. Mark the dart shape on the wrong

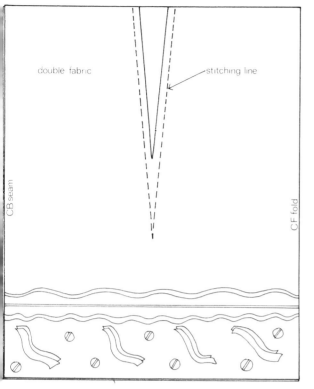

double fabric

stitching line

CB seam

CF fold

Fig 1

Making up: Join and finish the centre back seam. Turn up the hem and complete with Wundaweb.

Press the Vilene pocket shapes to the wrong side of one pair of fabric pockets.

Place each one to the edge of the cut out dart, right sides together, on the edge nearest the seam and with the top of the pocket 10 cm below the top of the skirt. Stitch, taking 5 mm turnings. Press joins open.

Attach the other two pocket pieces to the front edges of the dart 10 cm below the waist.

Fold fabric right-sides together and pin the dart to form a tapering seam.

Stitch from the waist to the point marked on the pocket edge. Close the pocket opening with stitching. Stitch from the base of the pocket to the point marked on the fabric below the cut dart. Neaten edges, press the dart open and flat. Complete the pocket. Neaten the top edge of the skirt and fold it over to form a casing 4 mm wider than the elastic. At the centre back seam, unpick the machine stitches for a little way to allow the casing to lie flat and to provide an opening for the elastic. Work a bar tack to prevent the stitching from coming undone further.

Press the casing and stitch, working two rows of machining.

Thread elastic or elastic petersham through the casing. Adjust to size and join.

Fitting: If you have a hollow back trim the waist edge to a curve between the side darts before making the casing.

Variations: Make the skirt mid-calf length.

Use plain fabric and make your own border with braid and embroidery or appliqué. Do this before marking or cutting the fabric.

Omit the pockets for speed.

Add patch pockets — taking the pattern from the Hooded Snuggler (p. 134).

Add a waistband in place of elastic. Decide on the width of the waistband and shorten the skirt by twice this amount. You may well be able to cut the band from wasted border design. Stitch the back seam but insert a 20 cm zip in the top of the seam. Complete the side darts and pockets then gather the waist edge on to the prepared waistband.

side of both layers. Cut out the dart on the lines (fig 1).

Fold the Vilene right-side out. Draw the shape of the pocket shown with pencil or felt pen. A plastic curve may help with the shape. The straight edge is 23 cm long then the bag curves down for a depth of 5 cm before curving upwards. On the straight edge mark a point 8 cm down as a guide for joining later. Cut out. Then cut four pieces in fabric (fig 2).

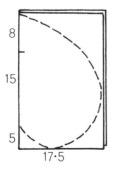

8

15

5

17·5

Fig 2

Slip-on dress

Soft, easy bias dress or nightdress in drapy fabric with drawn-up neck and waistline. Make long pieces of rouleau to thread through the neck and tie round the waist.

Quick to make, only four seams, the hem and the neckline.

Size: To fit up to 97 cm bust

Fig 1

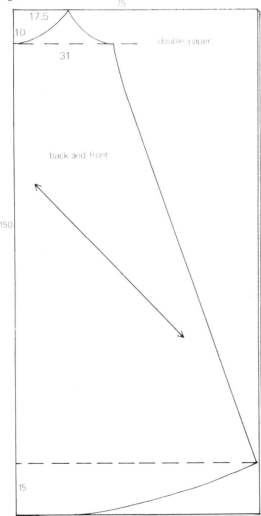

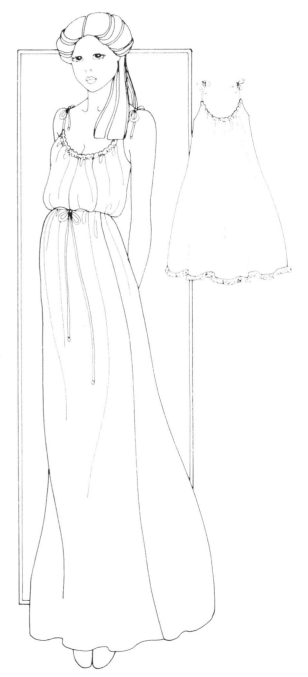

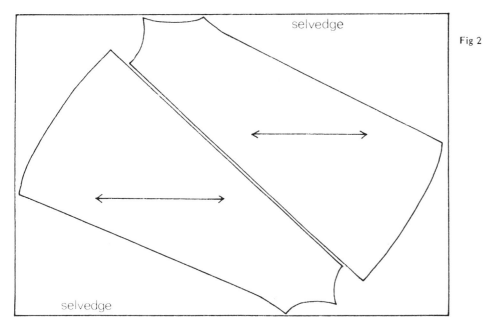

selvedge

selvedge

Fig 2

Length: Back neck to hem 145 cm (allowing 7 cm for blousing at waist).

Reduce the fullness in the dress by taking 3-4 cm off the pattern at the centre front and centre back.

Seam allowance: 1.5 cm
2 cm at hem

Fabric: Use light-weight jersey,
3.90 m of 140 cm fabric or
3.70 m of 150 cm fabric

The dress could also be made successfully in other fine soft fabrics such as voile, chiffon, georgette, crêpe but they may not be as wide. Buy extra fabric and cut out, allowing for a join near the hem.

You will need 4.40 m of 115 cm fabric

Haberdashery: 3 reels Drima
Small beads for the ends of the rouleau

The pattern: The back and front are alike. The pattern takes a piece of paper 75 cm wide and 150 cm long. Join sheets together. It will be easier to cut out the fabric if you have two pattern pieces, so use two sheets of paper, one on top of the other.

Copy the pattern shape shown starting 10 cm down from the fold. The under-arm point is 31 cm from the fold and from there the side seam is a straight line to a point 15 cm above the bottom of the paper. Curve the hem down to the fold and curve the top of the dress from the centre fold up to the top of the paper 17.5 cm in from the fold. From there curve down to the under-arm. A plastic curve may help (fig 1).

Mark the straight grain position at an angle of 45° across the pattern.

Cut out and separate the two pieces of pattern.

Cutting out: Fold the fabric right-side out, across the width. Make sure the selvedges and ends are together. Place the pattern pieces with the straight grain arrow parallel with the selvedge, pin and cut out (fig 2).

When using narrow fabric draw a line on the pattern marking where the selvedge cuts across. After cutting all pieces lay the pattern on the spare fabric and cut out the remaining triangles of pattern. Match the grain correctly and remember to allow a seam allowance along the straight edge to be seamed. After cutting out join these pieces to the main skirt.

Cut crossway strips from the surplus pieces of fabric. Cut 2 m for the neck drawstring, 2 m for the belt and sufficient to face the neck and armhole edges.

Making up: Stitch the centre and side seams. Using the crossway strip face or bind the armholes. Face the front and back neckline of the dress, finishing the ends of the crossway strip to leave a slot for threading the ties.

Make two lengths of rouleau ties and thread one through each neck casing.

Put the dress on, adjust and fasten the ties.

Make the rouleau tie belt. Wear it tied over the dress or mark the waistline and attach a casing to WS of the dress through which to thread the belt. Make the casing from another piece of crossway strip or a piece of bias binding, place it on WS of dress and stitch along each edge. Make two handsewn eyelets for the belt to emerge through.

Variations: Work rows of shirring to mark the waist and omit the belt.

Wear a narrow purchased belt.

Make a wider tie belt.

Shorten the pattern to mini length and make it as a disco dress, a slip or a nightdress.

Use ribbon instead of rouleau in the neck and attach lace to the hem.

Wrap skirt

Wrap skirt with waistband and stitched edges, it is fastened with Velcro to make it adjustable.

Size: To fit 97 cm hip

Length: 76 cm

Adjust the size by adding or subtracting a little at the centre back and sides of the pattern.

Seam allowance: 1.5 cm

        5 cm on hem

        7 cm allowed for fold-back facing on front of skirt

Fabric: Any light or medium fabric including wool and synthetics in woven or jersey construction, cotton, polyester and cotton, cord, denim.

    1.80 m of 140 or 150 cm fabric

Haberdashery: 3 reels Drima

        Petersham or interfacing for waist-band

        16 cm Velcro 3 cm wide

        85 cm Fold-a-Band

        Wundaweb

The pattern: You will need a piece of squared paper 85 cm long and 40 cm wide for the back. The edge on the left is the centre back and will be placed to the fold of the fabric. At the hem, the width of the skirt is 1 cm less than the size of the paper and the hem curves up to a point 2.5 cm above the bottom edge of the paper.

Rule a line across the paper 70 cm above the hemline at the centre back. Measure 26 cm along this line and rule from there down to the outer point of the hem (fig 1).

Measure 6 cm in along the horizontal line and mark a point directly above it but at the edge of the paper. Draw a slight curve from there to join the side line to complete the side seam.

Draw the waistline by first measuring 10 cm in from the side seam and 2.5 cm down and draw a curve. Rule a dart as shown, making it 1.5 cm wide, and coming to a point on the line below.

Complete the waist by drawing a curve from the dart to the centre back edge.

To make the front pattern use a piece of paper 85 cm long and 90 cm wide. Fold the paper under at a point 25 cm in from the right-hand edge. Write

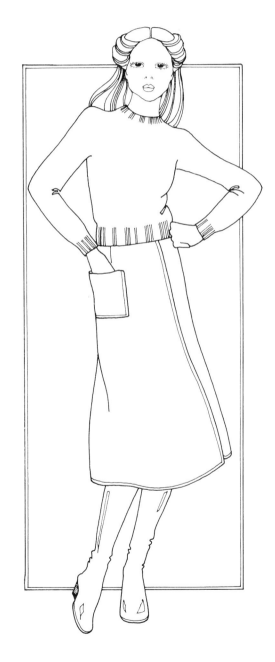

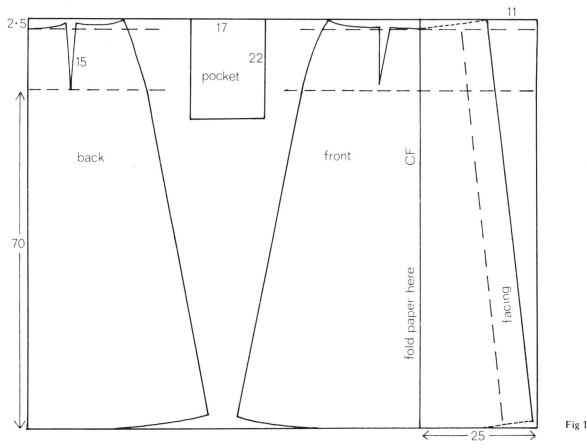

Fig 1

on the fold 'centre front' and put grain arrows on it.

At the bottom edge of the paper draw the hem in the same way as for the back.

Mark a line across the paper 70 cm above the hem and rule a straight side seam as for the back.

Measure in 5 cm on this line and curve in the remainder of the side seam up to the top edge of the paper.

Start the waistline curve by drawing a line dropping by 1 cm by the time it reaches the dart position 10 cm in. Make the dart 1 cm wide but it should stop short of the line below by 2 cm. Complete the waist curve by dropping the line to a point 2 cm below the top of the paper by the time it reaches the fold.

Cut out the pattern with the paper still folded. Open it out and shape the skirt wrap-over by ruling a straight line from the hem edge up to a point 11 cm in from the right-hand edge of the paper. Trim off the paper.

Cutting out: Place the pattern on the fabric folded as shown. Match the straight grain on the front. Pin and cut out (fig 2).

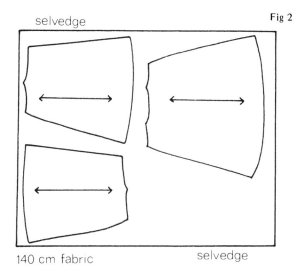

Fig 2

selvedge

140 cm fabric   selvedge

Mark the darts, the centre back, centre front and also mark the fold line of the front facing 7 cm inside the edge of the fabric.

Making up: Press Fold-a-Band to the wrong side of each skirt front, locating the perforations over the facing fold line. Neaten the raw edges of the facing extension (fig 3).

Fig 3

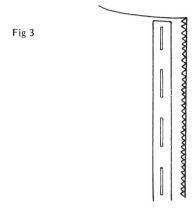

Place back skirt right-side up and front skirts on top right-side down, matching the side seams. Tack. Tack in the front and back darts. Try the skirt on, matching the centre front lines. Adjust if necessary. Attach pockets if desired — see *Variations.*

Complete the darts and side seams. Fold back the front facings and tack. Press. Make a straight or curved waistband and attach. Try on the skirt and mark the position of the wrap-over on the band. Mark the hemline.

Open out the front facing and turn up the hem. Fold facing back into position and hold back by inserting a length of Wundaweb between the skirt and the facing (fig 4).

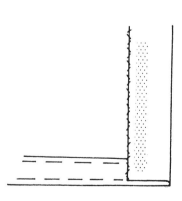

Fig 4

Work decorative stitching down front edge and round the hem. Attach the Velcro to the waistband. *Variations:* Before attaching waistband trim the seam allowance of the front edges and trim the hem off the bottom, enclose the raw edges in braid. Attach waistband.

Sew two large buttons to the outside of the waistband (fig 5).

Fig 5

Add a patch pocket. Attach it after stitching the darts and side seams. Place the top of it so that the right corner just covers the point of the dart.

Insert seam pockets. Use the pattern given for the Single-Seam Skirt (p. 112) and attach them to the side seams 10 cm below the waist edge, before stitching the side seams.

Vary the length of the skirt — cut it only 50 cm long, trim it with ric-rac braid or embroidery. Alternatively attach long ends of braid or contrasting fabric to the waistband and to the skirt and tie (this is in addition to the Velcro). Wear it for sports and holidays. Team it with the sleeveless version of the Sweater (p. 128), the whole outfit in cotton jersey, towelling, velour, track suit fabric, etc.

Lengthen the pattern to ankle length and make the skirt in soft cotton, light-weight jersey or panne velvet.

Tunic

Fig 1

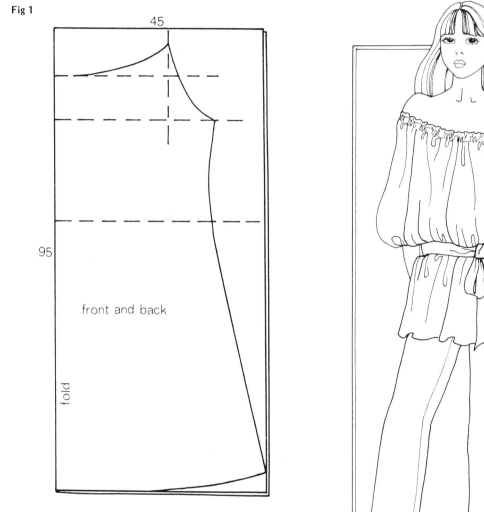

45

95

front and back

fold

Loose tunic with elastic or drawstring neck. Lift with a hipline sash and wear it with the Trousers (p. 131). Very quick to make with raglan sleeves, elastic in the wrists and machined hem.

Size: 10-14

Length: 92 cm

Adjust by adding or subtracting a small amount at the centre edge of the pattern.

Seam allowance: 1.5 cm
2 cm at hem, neck and sleeve hems

Fabric: 2.60 m of 115 cm jersey fabric, or 2.40 m if it is 150 cm or more wide

Haberdashery: 2 reels Drima (3 if fluting the hem)
1.50 m narrow elastic for neck
50 cm narrow elastic for sleeves
Shirring elastic for waist

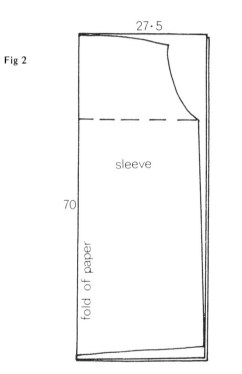

Fig 2

The pattern: The front and back are the same so cut one pattern piece. The diagram shows half the sleeve so draw it on a folded piece of paper.

For the main pattern piece use a piece of paper 45 cm wide and 95 cm long. Begin at the bottom left and mark the hemline, curving it up to a point 5 cm above the bottom of the paper.

Measure 55 cm up the left-hand edge of the paper and rule a line across. Mark a point 34 cm along and draw the side seam from there to the hem. Curve the line in slightly for 5 cm then gently out for 10 cm before ruling the remainder with a ruler (fig 1).

Rule a horizontal line across the paper 21 cm over the first, another 9 cm above that and a vertical one 24 cm in from the left-hand edge.

Curve the armhole and neckline as shown and complete the side seam.

To make the sleeve pattern fold a piece of paper 55 cm wide and 70 cm long (fig 2).

At the bottom of the folded edge measure up 4 cm and from there curve the hemline to a point 5 cm above the bottom of the paper by the time it reaches the edge of the paper.

Rule a sleeve seam 48 cm long from this point but slope it in 1 cm.

At the top of the paper rule a horizontal line 19 cm long 2 cm down. Curve the top of the sleeve as shown and from there curve the armhole.

Cutting out: Cut out the front and back and two sleeves with the straight grain of the fabric running down the centre of each (fig 3).

If making a sash from matching fabric cut it from the surplus piece.

Making up: Stitch tunic side seams and sleeve seams.

Turn up a 2 cm hem at the bottom of the sleeves and stitch to form a casing.

Set sleeves into armholes, matching sleeve seam to tunic side seam.

Turn in a 2 cm hem round the neck and tops of sleeves and stitch to form a casing. Insert elastic

Fig 3

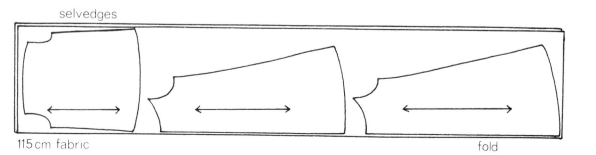

Fig 4

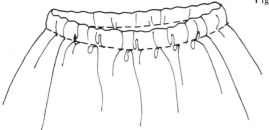

and pin. Try on dress and adjust elastic. Mark the waistline, blousing the tunic as much as desired (fig 4).

Join the elastic. Work several rows of shirring round the waistline and insert elastic in the sleeves. Machine the hem. Make the sash.

Variations: Insert ribbon in the neckline instead of elastic.

Shorten the sleeves to elbow length or shorter.

Leave short sleeves loose without elastic.

Lengthen the pattern to dress length.

Fabric: 3.20 m of 115 cm fabric or 2.70 m of 150 cm fabric.

Robe

Wrap-over robe with bands and wide sleeves, and fold-back cuffs. A comfortable all-purpose garment.

Size: 14-16

Length: Back neck to hem 145 cm

Adjust width by adding or subtracting small amounts at the centre back and side seams of the pattern.

Seam allowance: 1.5 cm
      5 cm on hem

Fabric: Use velour, stretch towelling, plush or other jersey fabric of 150 cm width

Haberdashery: 2 reels Drima
      Fold-a-Band for cuffs

The pattern: You will need pieces of paper 155 cm long for the back and front patterns, join sheets to obtain this length.

For the back pattern use a piece of paper 35 cm wide. Begin at the bottom and mark the hemline, curving it up to a point 1 cm above the edge of the paper (fig 1).

Draw a line across the paper 110 cm above the hem and measure across it 30 cm. Draw the side seam from the hem to this point and then curve it out by 1 cm to a point 10 cm above.

At the top of the paper measure down 6 cm and draw a horizontal line. Mark the end of the shoulder seam 29 cm along it. Draw the armhole as shown. Draw the neckline 9 cm wide starting 4 cm below the top of the paper and curving up 2 cm. Complete the shoulder seam.

To draw the front pattern take a piece of paper 155 cm long and 50 cm wide. Fold under the edge on the right turning 15 cm underneath. The folded edge of paper is the centre front. Mark it as such and put grain arrows on it.

At the bottom of the paper measure across from the right 32 cm and draw a curved hemline. Mark horizontal guide lines on the paper 110, 10 and 30 cm above this. Draw the lower part of the side seam sloping it in to a point 29 cm from the centre front. Curve it more as shown for the last 10 cm. Above this, curve the seam out again for 1 cm to the line above.

Measure along the top guide line 29 cm and from

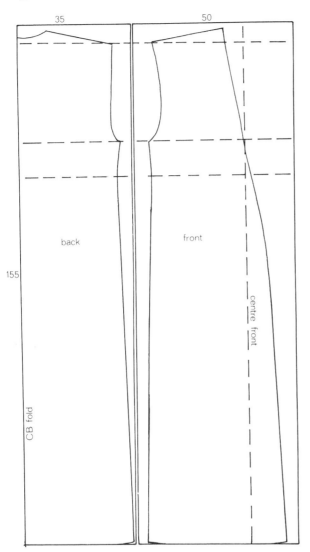

Fig 1

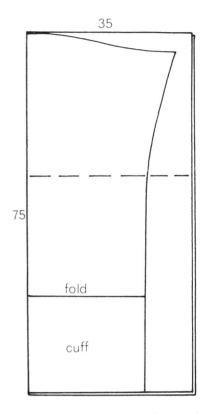

Fig 2

there draw the armhole in a curve as shown.

Measure along the top edge of the paper 6 cm and start the shoulder seam line 1.5 cm below this.

The neckline runs in a slightly concave curve from that point down to the next guide line, joining the guide line exactly on the fold of the paper.

Open out the paper and continue curving the front edge but now slightly convex for 30 cm before completing it, using a ruler. This line should meet the bottom of the paper 4 cm in from the edge.

To make the sleeve pattern fold a piece of paper 70 cm wide and 75 cm long. Measure from the fold 25 cm along the bottom edge. From there draw a line up to a point 45 cm above the hem. Draw the sleeve head as shown sloping it down to a point 3.5

cm below the top of the paper and 3 cm in from the edge. From there complete the sleeve seam as shown. Cut out and open the paper for the complete sleeve pattern (fig 2).

Draw a line across the pattern 20 cm above the hem to mark the fold line for the cuff.

Cutting out: Place the back to a fold. Cut the front and sleeve with the straight grain running lengthwise (fig 3).

Cut two bands for the edges 164 cm long and 12 cm wide.

For the belt cut a piece of fabric, or pieces to join, 12 cm wide and 160 cm long.

Making up: Join the shoulder seams, reinforcing them to prevent stretching.

Press Fold-a-Band to the wrong side of each sleeve, locating the perforations over the cuff fold line (fig 4).

Insert the sleeves into the armholes. Join the sleeve and side seam in one continuous seam.

Turn up the sleeve hem on the Fold-a-Band and stitch the edge of the cuff to the sleeve. Turn back the cuffs and hold in position with three bar tacks worked between the cuff and the sleeve (fig 5).

Turn up and complete the hem.

Join the two bands, fold the strip in half with wrong sides together and attach to the edges of the robe as a double fabric edge. At the hem of the robe

selvedges

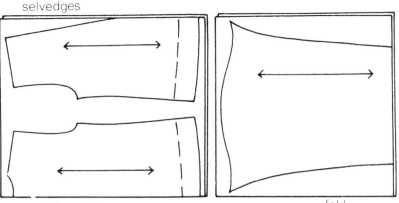

Fig 3

140 or 150cm fabric

fold

Fig 4

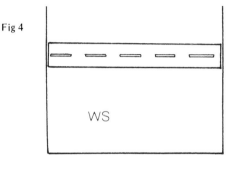

WS

turn in the end level with the hem before folding the band (fig 6).

Make two fabric belt loops and attach at the waist. Also make a fabric hanger and attach to the back of the neck.

Variations: Add pockets. Use the patch pocket given for the Wrap Skirt (p. 117) or add seam pockets using the pattern from the Single-Seam Skirt (p. 112).

Sew a small piece of Velcro at the waist where the robe wraps over to stop it from falling open (fig 7).

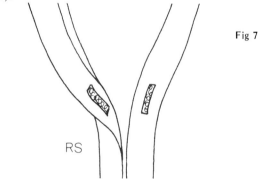

Fig 7

RS

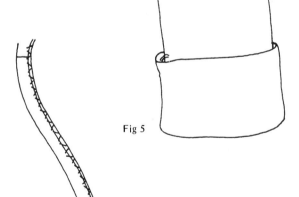

Fig 5

RS

Fig 6

Shorten the pattern by 75 cm to thigh length, and team it with trousers. Make bands and belts in contrasting fabric. The jacket could be made in a wide variety of fabrics including crêpe, polyester and cottom, satin, panne velvet.

Fabric: 3 m of 90 cm fabric
        2 m of 140 or 150 cm fabric plus extra if contrast is used

Use jersey, wool or synthetic coating, brushed fabrics to make a cardigan.

Fabric: 2 m of 140 or 150 cm fabric

Omit the sleeves and bands, re-shape the front edge so that is does not extend beyond the centre front and make a warm waistcoat from fur fabric, brushed coating, blanket cloth, etc., finish the edges with the braid and add braid ties.

Fabric: 1 m of 140 or 150 cm fabric

Bias skirt and shawl

A pretty skirt cut on the cross with a quickly made matching shawl. The skirt has pockets and is gathered into a waistband.

There is a concealed zip in the centre back seam.

Size: To fit 71 cm waist

Length: 76 cm

To reduce or increase the size adjust the pattern at the centre front and centre back.

Seam allowance: 1.5 cm
        2 cm hem

Fabric: Use any plain or checked medium-weight fabric. If woven fabric is used the shawl edges can be fringed, if jersey fabric is used attach bought fringe (5.70 m).

  2.40 of 140 cm wide fabric or

  2.20 of 150 cm wide fabric

Haberdashery: 2 reels Drima

      Petersham or stiffening for waistband

      Velcro or hooks, trouser clips to fasten

      20 cm concealed zip

Fig 1

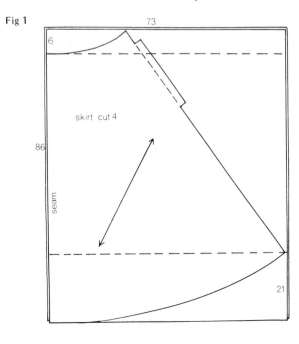

73

6

skirt cut 4

86

seam

21

selvedge

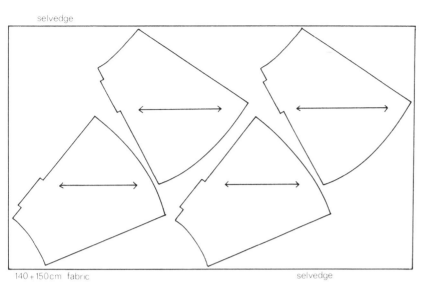

140 + 150 cm fabric   selvedge

Iron-on Vilene (Softline), 30 cm x 40 cm for the pockets

The pattern: You will need one piece of paper 73 cm wide by 86 cm deep. The front and back skirt pattern pieces are the same but as only half the pattern is shown it helps when you come to cutting out if you make two copies of the pattern — use two pieces of paper (fig 1).

Begin at the bottom left and draw in the hemline. Draw an even curve to a point 21 cm above the bottom of the paper.

Draw a horizontal guide line across the paper 6 cm below the top edge and mark a point 25 cm along. Curve in the waistline as shown. From the side waist point rule a straight line to the hem. Add 1.5 cm to the side seam where the pockets will be attached so that the join will not be obvious if checked fabric is used. Begin the extension 5 cm below the waist and make it 28 cm in length.

Fold the Vilene in half and draw the pocket shape from the Single-Seam Skirt (p. 112) on it with pencil or felt pen. Mark a point 8 cm below the top to indicate the opening. Cut out.

Cutting out: Place the pattern pieces on single fabric and pin with the straight grain positioned as shown. Cut out.

Cut four pocket pieces using the Vilene as a guide (fig 2).

Cut a square of fabric 140 cm x 140 cm for the shawl.

Making up: Mark the centre back and centre front. Stitch and press centre back and centre front seams. Insert the zip in the back seam. Press the Vilene to the wrong side of two of the pocket pieces. Attach these to the extensions on the back skirt. Press.

Attach the other two pocket pieces to the front extensions.

Join the side seams, closing up the pocket opening with stitching. Complete the seams and the pockets.

Insert a gathering thread in the skirt waist or make small unpressed pleats.

Cut and interface a waistband and attach it, gathering the skirt to fit. Attach fastenings to the waistband.

Try on the skirt and mark the hemline. Turn up and complete the hem.

Pull fibres from all edges of the shawl to make a fringe of a suitable depth. Work zig-zag stitch round the edge of the fabric to prevent further fibres coming away (fig 3).

If using jersey fabric turn a narrow hem all round and machine it. Attach the fringe by hand or machine.

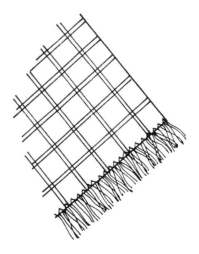

Fig 3

Sweater

Fig 1

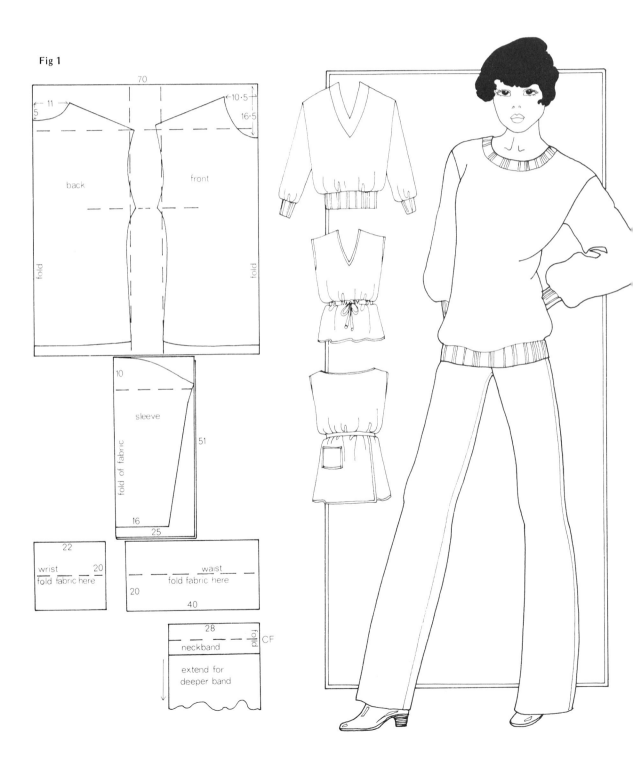

70

11 · 10.5

5 · 16.5

back · front

fold · fold

10

sleeve

fold of fabric

51

16

25

22

wrist · 20

fold fabric here

20

waist

fold fabric here

40

28

neckband

fold CF

extend for
deeper band

Fig 2

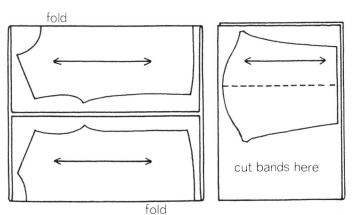

fold

cut bands here

fold

140 or 150 cm fabric

A loose blouson jersey top with extended shoulder and bands of fabric or ribbing at neck, cuffs and hem. It can be made in a couple of hours.

Size: 14-16

Length: 67 cm

For a smaller size take small amounts from centre back, centre front and side seams of pattern. Re-draw the side seams and armholes within the line shown following the original shape.

Seam allowance: The usual 1.5 cm has been allowed on all edges, but if you are using one of the narrow seams suitable for jersey this can be reduced to 4 mm before cutting out in fabric.

Fabric: Use medium to thick knits and jersey including velour, track suit fabric, stretch towelling, panne velvet, plush, fancy knit fabrics, fur fabric. Use self fabric or ribbed knit fabric or hand knitting for the bands.

1.40 m of either 140 cm or 150 cm fabric, or 1.20 m if contrast ribbing is used.

Haberdashery: 2 reels Drima
45 cm narrow ribbon, tape or seam binding for shoulder seams.

The pattern: You will need a piece of paper 70 cm wide and 80 cm deep to draw the front and back sweater pattern. Only half the sleeve pattern is shown. Either fold the fabric, chalk the pattern as shown directly on to the fabric and cut out (cut two sleeves in this way), or fold a piece of paper 50 cm wide and 51 cm deep and draw the sleeve pattern (fig 1).

The bands for neck, wrists and hem can be cut directly in fabric.

Draw the hemline for the back and front 3 cm above the edge of the paper, curving it up slightly to a point 30 cm in. From there draw a vertical line to the top of the paper. Draw the side seams sloping in slightly and then curving out and beyond the marker line 43 cm above the bottom of the paper.

Draw a marker line 13 cm below the top of the paper. Draw in the back neckline 10 cm down curving to 11 cm in and rule a 22 cm shoulder seam from there onto the marker line below.

The front neckline starts 16.5 cm down and curves up to 10.5 cm in. Rule the shoulder seam but note that it joins the armhole curve 1.5 cm above the marker line.

To draw half the sleeve mark the hemline 16 cm long 4 cm above the bottom of the paper. Rule a marker line 10 cm below the top and rule the sleeve seam. Above that point draw a slightly angled line 2 cm long before curving the sleeve head as shown. The curve is slightly concave for 10 cm but convex for the top of the arm.

Cutting out: Fold the fabric sides to middle and cut the back and front to a fold. Re-fold the remainder of the fabric in order to cut the sleeves and bands (fig 2).

Cut pieces of ribbing or fabric to sizes shown to fold double for attaching.

Making up: Stitch shoulder seams, using a slight zig-zag stitch or one of the narrow or stretch seams. Insert tape to prevent stretching.

Insert sleeves, placing centre of sleeve head to shoulder seam with right sides together; ease sleeve to fit armhole and stitch the seam.

Stitch side seam and sleeve seam in one operation.

Join all bands, fold them wrong sides together and attach. The full sleeve will have to be gathered to the ribbing or fabric. The neck and hem bands

Fig 3

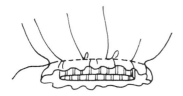

need stretching slightly to fit (fig 3).

Variations: Cut a V neck and attach a double band of fabric.

Cut a piece of ribbing or fabric 50 cm deep for the round neck and attach it as a cowl.

Omit the sleeves, cut a V neck, bind the neck and armholes with self fabric; shorten the pattern by 15 cm and insert a drawstring through a casing at the waist. Made in light-weight jersey, it is a perfect top to go with the Single-Seam Skirt (p.112), the Wrap Skirt (p.117) or the Bias Skirt (p.126).

Trousers

Easy trousers with straight leg, elastic or drawstring in waist. Wear with any of the tops shown in the book.

Size: 16
Length at side seam: 107 cm
Width of leg at hem: 54 cm

For smaller sizes reduce the pattern at side seams by the following amounts:

    For size 10 − 32 mm
    For size 12 − 22 mm
    For size 14 − 12 mm

Also re-shape the crutch seam as shown for each size.

Fig 1

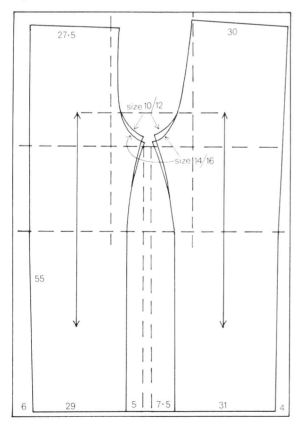

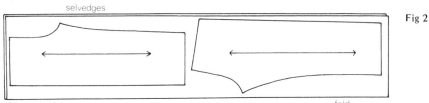

Fig 2

selvedges

90 + 115 cm fabric   fold

selvedges

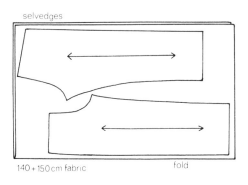

140 + 150 cm fabric   fold

To adjust the leg length alter at the hem.

Seam allowance: 1.5 cm

3 cm at waist

4 cm at hem

Fabric: Use any light-weight woven or jersey fabric, including cotton, satin, viscose, ciré, synthetic jersey, panne velvet, velour, stretch towelling, velveteen.

2.40 m of 90 cm fabric or

2.40 m of 115 cm fabric or

1.50 m of 140 cm fabric or

1.30 m of 150 cm fabric

Haberdashery: 2 reels Drima

80 cm elastic 20 mm wide

The pattern: You will have to join pieces of paper to make a piece 120 cm long and 85 cm wide.

Draw the hemline of back and front legs 2 cm above the bottom edge. Mark off the leg widths as shown. Draw perpendicular guide lines for the inside leg and 82 cm long. Draw the inside leg and outside leg seams straight up to 55 cm from the bottom of the paper then shape as shown (fig 1).

To draw the crutch seam, rule perpendicular guide lines at 30 cm and 55 cm measuring from the left-hand edge of the paper.

The front seam drops straight almost to the guide line below before curving out to meet the inside leg seam. The back crutch starts higher and slopes out by 5 cm before curving to the inside leg. Follow whichever curve is appropriate to the size you are making.

Cutting out: Follow the diagram for cutting out (fig 2).

Making up: Arrange the front legs on a table with right sides up and place the back legs on top right-sides down. Match up the outside leg edges and join. Match the inside leg edges and join (fig 3).

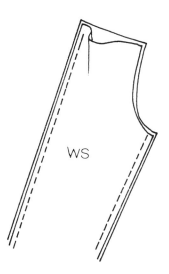

WS

Fig 3

Fig 4

With legs right-side out, pin in side leg seams together (fig 4).

Turn over 3 cm at the waist and machine to form a casing. Cut elastic to size and insert. Join securely.

Turn up hems and adjust length. Make a deep hem or a Wundaweb hem.

Variations: Use cord or rouleau instead of elastic.

Make the hems into stitched casings and insert cord ties or elastic.

Pleat the waist into a waistband: reduce the height at the waist by 1.5 cm, insert a 20 cm zip in the front seam, and add a waistband. The band can be fastened conventionally or it can have long ties.

Hooded snuggler

Neither a cape nor a poncho but a warm, loose casual thing to snuggle into. One piece of fabric — no shoulder seams — a hood, pockets and braid round the edges.

Size: All sizes

Length: 112 cm

Seam allowance: 1.5 cm. No allowance at outer edge as braid is to be attached.

Fabric: Any thick, spongy fabric, including coating, blanket cloth, mohair, reversible cloth. Unsuitable for one-way fabrics.

2.70 m of 140 or 150 cm fabric

Haberdashery: 2 reels Drima

                5.50 m braid 4 cm wide

                7 toggle buttons

The pattern: This is a simple shape that can easily be drawn on the fabric. Fold the fabric and find the half-way point along the fold. Mark the shoulder line then draw the neckline. Cut it out and cut down the centre front fold for 29 cm for the neck opening (fig 1).

At the far side mark the points for attaching the buttons at the sides. They are 10 cm in from the edge of the fabric and 32 cm down from the shoulder at the front and 40 cm at the back.

The edge of the snuggler is parallel with this line and then curves round to 30 cm from the fold. From there draw a straight hemline.

The pocket position is 15 cm below the neck slit and 10 cm from the centre front.

For the hood pattern you will need a piece of paper 31 cm wide and 45 cm deep. Use the patch pocket pattern from the Wrap Skirt (p. 117) but cut it larger by 2 cm all round (fig 2).

Cutting out: Cut the main part in fabric. Cut two hood sections. Cut two pockets.

Making up: Attach braid to outer edge.

Make and attach the pockets.

Stitch the centre back seam of the hood as a welt seam.

Join hood to neckline with a welt seam.

Bind the face edge of the hood and the slit neckline (fig 3).

Make braid loops and attach to the right side of

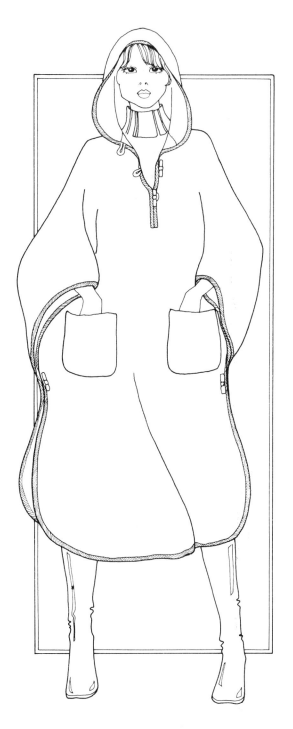

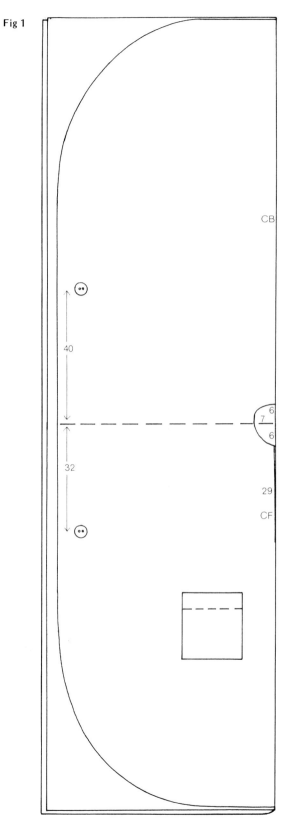

Fig 1

the opening. Sew buttons to correspond with the loops. Sew pairs of buttons to hold the sides closed. *Variations:* Make ties from the braid instead of loops and buttons.

Turn machined hems instead of using braid. Shorten the pattern by 30 cm for a short version.

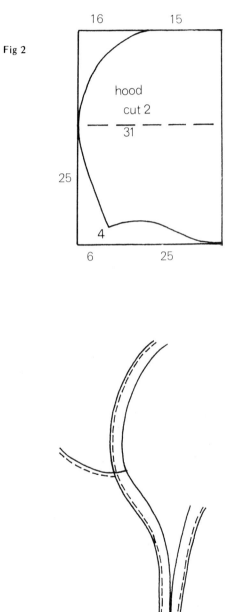

Fig 2

hood
cut 2

Fig 3

Zip jacket

A hip-length blouson with chunky zip and collar. This includes more processes than any other design but the extended shoulder and elastic wrists and hem make it easy to get a good result.

Can be worn with the Trousers (p. 131), in which case put elastic or cord through the hems.

Size: 12-14

For a smaller size take equal amounts from centre front and centre back.

Length: Back neck to hem 64 cm

Seam allowance: 1.5 cm
                  3 cm on hems

Fabric: Velour, jersey velvet, panne velvet, velveteen, needlecord, corduroy, nylon ciré, proofed poplin, stretch towelling, candlewick, cotton jersey.

1.40 m of 150 cm fabric

Haberdashery: 2 reels Drima
                   Small piece iron-on Vilene 48 x 15 cm for collar e.g. Softline
                   1.50 m elastic 1 cm wide
                   60 cm open-ended nylon zip or big Alpine zip

The pattern: For the back you need a piece of squared paper 35 cm wide and 80 cm deep. Draw in the hemline, curving it up slightly to finish at a point 2 cm before the edge of the paper. Measure 44 cm up the edge of the paper to find the armhole level. Draw in the side seam sloping in 5 cm (fig 1).

Draw the neckline 11 cm down and 10 cm in at the top corner. Rule the shoulder yoke seam 19 cm long, sloping down to 10 cm below the top of the paper. Curve the armhole as shown. The top 15 cm slope gently but under the arm it dips sharply from the side seam before starting to rise.

For the front use a piece of paper 35 cm wide and 70 cm deep. Rule in the hemline as shown, 4 cm above the bottom of the paper but curve it up slightly. The under-arm level is 47 cm up from the bottom of the paper. Rule the side seam, sloping it in 4 cm.

The neckline is a curve 5 cm deep by 5 cm wide. The outer point of the shoulder yoke seam is 9 cm down and 7 cm in from the edge of the paper. Curve the seam from there to the neck point.

Mark two tucks 3 cm wide and 2 cm apart in the middle of that seam.

For the sleeve fold a piece of paper 70 cm deep and 50 cm wide to draw half the sleeve. Draw the sleeve head to a point 14 cm down, curving the top 10 cm gently, the next 5 cm at a slant and the last 10 cm should be slightly concave. Cut out the sleeve head shape, open out the pattern for the complete sleeve.

Cutting out: Fold the fabric and place the back to the fold with the front beside it on the selvedge. Pin the sleeve below the front and cut out.

Cut the collar from the remainder still with the fabric double. The collar is 15 cm deep and 24 cm long. The fold of the fabric becomes the centre back of the collar.

Pockets may be cut from the remainder. They should be 30 cm deep and 20 cm wide.

Making up: Pin the tucks, folding the fabric out towards the armhole. Join the front and back shoulders with an overlaid seam or handle as a welt seam (fig 2).

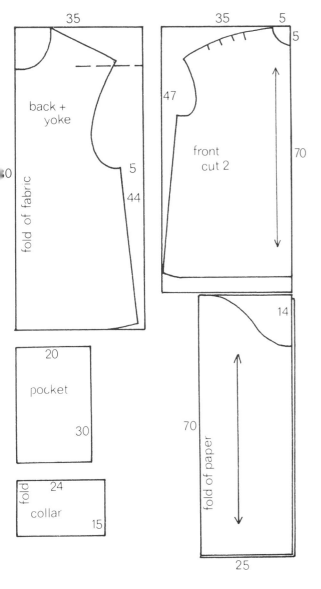

Fig 1

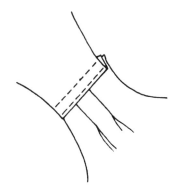

Fig 2

Insert the sleeves, easing the sleeve into the arm-hole.

Stitch the sleeve and side seam in one move-ment (fig 3).

Fig 3

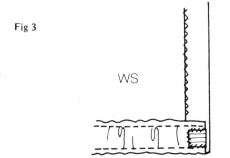

Turn up the sleeve hems. Turn up the hems of the jacket. Insert elastic.

Insert the zip. Attach the collar to the neckline, following the single layer method for shirt collars. *Variations:* Attach the patch pockets after cutting out but before working any processes.

Place the pockets 6 cm above the hemline and 3 cm from the centre front edge (fig 4).

Use cord to drawstring the hem.

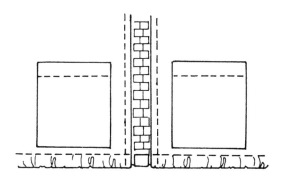

Fig 4

Hat and scarf

Pull-on hat and long scarf. A classic set quick to make but to be worn with practically anything.

Size: All sizes

Fabric: Only suitable for stretchy knitted fabrics
   80 cm of 140 or 150 cm fabric
   50 cm fringe or knitting yarn to make fringe

Haberdashery: 1 reel Drima

The pattern: Both scarf and hat are simple rectangles that can be cut from fabric to the sizes shown in the diagram (fig 1).

Cutting out: Cut all pieces across the width of the fabric.

Making up: Fold hat section in half and join the seam. Fold tube wrong-sides together and gather up the crown edges separately, drawing them together and tucking in the raw ends of fabric. Fold edge back to form brim. Narrow elastic such as shirring elastic could be inserted in the fabric at the fold to tighten the hat (fig 2).

Fig 1

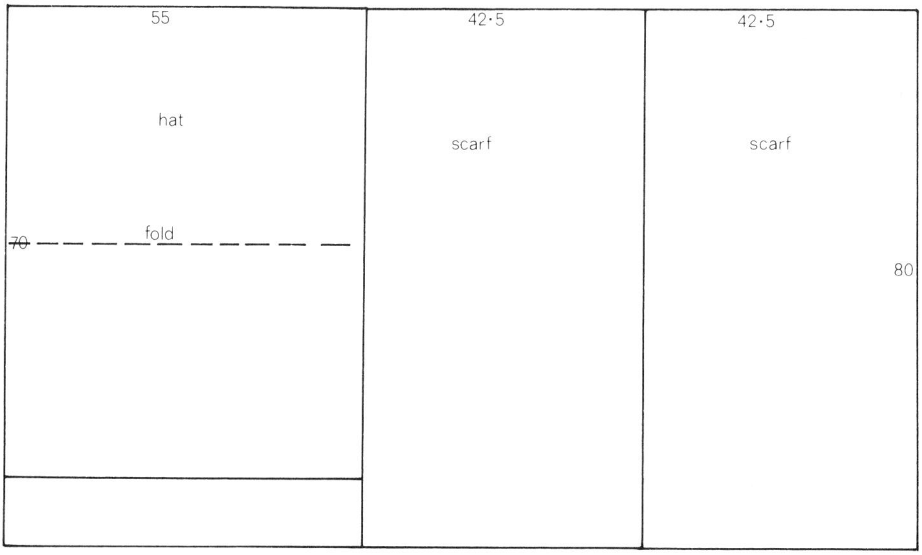

55	42·5	42·5
hat	scarf	scarf
70 — — — fold — — — —		80

Fig 2

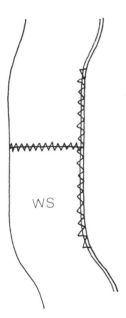

folded edge

Join the scarf pieces end to end. Fold in half lengthwise and stitch to form a tube (fig 3).

Turn right side out. Attach fringe to ends.

Variation: Cut scarf longer and tie ends in a knot.

WS

Fig 3

Bag

Simple tote bag style. Use as a handbag or general carrying bag.

Fabric: Use any strong, stiff fabric such as canvas, hessian, heavy PVC, ticking, deck chair canvas, calico, or a softer fabric and back it before making with firm iron-on Vilene.

    1.10 m of fabric 45 cm wide or
    55 cm of 90 cm fabric

Haberdashery: 1 reel Drima
                 3.80 m webbing 2.5 cm wide
                 Stiff card and thin foam sheet

The pattern: Cut the bag from double fabric to the size shown. Mark off 10 cm at the bottom corners as shown and also mark the position of the webbing (fig 1).

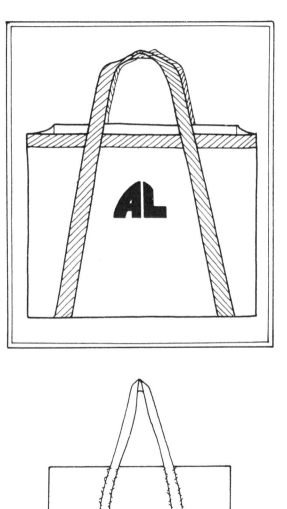

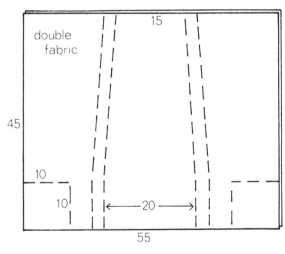

Fig 1

Making up: Attach the webbing handles (fig 2).

    Stitch the four corners by folding the fabric right-sides together, matching the marks and stitching as a dart.

    Make a seam across the base of the bag and up each side in one operation (fig 3).

Fig 2

Fig 3

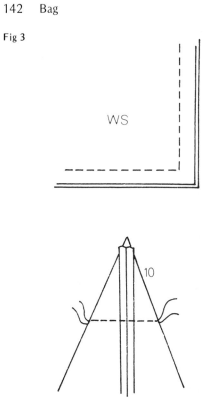

WS

Fig 4

Fold across base seam and stitch as a dart 10 cm from the point (fig 4).

Cut a piece of strong card 35 cm long and 20 cm wide. Slip it into the base of the bag and trim it to fit easily. Glue a piece of foam sheeting to one side and cover the whole with an odd piece of fabric or with sheet plastic.

Index